Critical Guides to German Texts

16 Brecht: Leben des Galilei

Critical Guides to German Texts

EDITED BY MARTIN SWALES

BRECHT

Leben des Galilei

John J. White

**Professor of German and Comparative Literature
King's College London**

Grant & Cutler Ltd
1996

© Grant & Cutler Ltd 1996

ISBN 0 7293 0391 8

DEPÓSITO LEGAL: V. 355 - 1997

Printed in Spain by
Artes Gráficas Soler, S.A., Valencia
for
GRANT & CUTLER LTD
55-57 GREAT MARLBOROUGH STREET, LONDON, W1V 2AY

Contents

Contents

Textual Note

Bertolt Brecht's Galilei play exists in three separate versions, the first and last in German, the middle one in English. These are:

(i) *Leben des Galilei*, 1938-39 (the 'Danish' *Urfassung*)
(ii) *Galileo*, 1947 (the 'Californian' version)
(iii) *Leben des Galilei*, 1955-56 (the 'Berlin' version).

The following Critical Guide will be based on the final, 'Berlin' version: *Leben des Galilei*, published in the Edition Suhrkamp (Vol. 1, Frankfurt a. M., 1962, same pagination in all subsequent reprints). Page references to this edition will be given in brackets after quotations.

References to Brecht's other works will, whenever possible, be to: *Gesammelte Werke* (Werkausgabe Edition Suhrkamp), 20 vols, Frankfurt a. M., 1967, using the abbreviation *GW* plus volume and page number.

Material not available in the Suhrkamp paperback edition of Brecht's *Gesammelte Werke*, including the Danish and Californian versions of *Leben des Galilei* and the companion 'Modellbuch' to the play, will be quoted from the current definitive edition-in-progress: Bertolt Brecht, *Große kommentierte Berliner und Frankfurter Ausgabe*, ed. Werner Hecht et al., 30 projected vols (Frankfurt a. M., Suhrkamp, 1980ff.). The abbreviated reference for this edition will be *BFA* plus volume and page number. All other references, indicated in brackets after quotations by an italicized number, are to the items listed in the Select Bibliography at the end of this book, followed by the page number.

1. Introduction: The Stages of a Critical Project

'We may be the last generation of the human species on earth,' Brecht declared in 1947 to the US House Committee on Un-American Activities (*13*, p.482). Yet despite the fact that the inhabitants of what Galilei calls 'unsere winzige Erde' have acquired the means to destroy the entire planet, there has been scant cultural reflection on the moral dilemmas posed by such a deadly capacity. Set in seventeenth-century Italy and dealing with an outwardly different set of issues from the agenda determined by the feasibility of nuclear extermination, *Leben des Galilei* nevertheless remains the most momentous response in German literature to what Brecht identified as 'das "atomarische Zeitalter"' (*16*, p.10).

'Unsere Aufführung', the author remarked of his second (American) version, 'fiel in die Zeit und das Land, wo eben die Atombombe hergestellt und militärisch verwertet worden war. [...] Der Tag des Abwurfs wird jedem, der ihn in den Staaten erlebt hat, schwer vergeßlich sein' (*18*, p.108). Brecht's concern is, nevertheless, not with the strategic significance of the bomb's deployment, ending, as it did, the hostilities in the Far East. Nor is it with the metaphysical *Angst* which the new weapon engendered, although it by and large raised the same issues of theodicy as the concentration camps had. For the Marxist Brecht, the bomb was first and foremost a socio-political phenomenon; 'die atombombe hat [...] die beziehungen zwischen gesellschaft und wissenschaft zu einem leben-und-tod-problem gemacht' (*1*, p.755). It is characteristic of the man that while most writers felt able to ignore such a life-or-death subject, Brecht could not.

Although the bomb is not specifically mentioned in the play, it has undoubtedly dominated the reception of *Leben des Galilei* over the last half-century. This is hardly surprising since the version we shall be concentrating on makes its underlying relevance to the

nuclear debate clear, above all in Scene 14, where Galilei presents
Andrea with a nightmarish prognosis of the threats generated by
technological progress combined with a lack of political maturity:

> Wenn   Wissenschaftler,   eingeschüchtert   durch
> selbstsüchtige Machthaber, sich damit begnügen, Wissen
> um des Wissens willen aufzuhäufen, kann die
> Wissenschaft zum Krüppel gemacht werden, und eure
> neuen Maschinen mögen nur neue Drangsale bedeuten.
> Ihr mögt mit der Zeit alles entdecken, was es zu
> entdecken gibt, und euer Fortschritt wird doch nur ein
> Fortschreiten von der Menschheit weg sein. Die Kluft
> zwischen euch und ihr kann eines Tages so groß werden,
> daß euer Jubelschrei über irgendeine neue
> Errungenschaft von einem universalen Entsetzensschrei
> beantwortet werden könnte. (pp.125f.)

Although the world was only just waking up to the dilemma
Galilei conjures up when these words were inserted into the play, our
own segment of the century has reached it with a vengeance. As Jim
Hiley's account of the 1980 London production put it: 'By the time
Galileo finally hauled itself on to the stage of the Olivier Theatre, its
clear references to nuclear weaponry had a pointed topical reference
in the debate about Cruise missiles' (*19*, p.3). Brecht's examination of
the ethics of scientific discovery has with some justice come to stand
as our age's ultimate dangerous-science parable, encompassing both a
vivid dramatization of the political situation that led to Hiroshima
and Nagasaki, combined, in the author's own ideological terms at
least, with an implied political solution. In fact, as we shall see, both
diagnosis and remedy are equally products of Brecht's Marxism. One
cannot do justice to such a work by divorcing it from his politics. It is
one thing not to condone his ideological position (nowadays, in our
post-communist age, the majority will not); but it is quite another
thing to deny the creative centrality of his Marxism or misrepresent
Brecht as being at heart no more than an enlightened humanist,
usually on the assumption that good writing should go hand in hand

with acceptable values or on the grounds that communism has been doubly discredited: by the Stalinist excesses of the author's own time and by more recent events. The play's politics were, and remain, an integral ingredient, not some icing on the cake.

The *Leben des Galilei* we tend to think of in the context of Hiroshima was, however, not originally conceived in response to the nuclear age. Nor could it have been. The November 1938 *Urfassung* well pre-dates not only the first use of atomic weapons, but even public knowledge of the advances in nuclear physics that made their creation possible. Hahn and Straßmann were not to observe nuclear fission in uranium until December 1938, and the military significance of their discovery did not percolate into public consciousness for some time. In its original form, Brecht's play was a product of the years when Hitler's *Wehrmacht* threatened the entire European continent, rather than of the closing phase of World War Two when America's destruction of two Japanese cities decisively terminated the fighting in the Far East, which had proved so costly in lives and suffering. According to its author, *Leben des Galilei* was conceived 'in jenen finsteren letzten Monaten [...], als viele den Vormarsch des Faschismus für unaufhaltsam und den endgültigen Zusammenbruch der westlichen Zivilisation für gekommen hielten' (*16*, p.16). It represented a response to an ominous chain of events triggered off by the very country which Brecht had been obliged to leave to go into exile: Hitler-Germany's *Anschluß* with Austria, the occupation of the Sudetenland, and the ill-fated Munich Agreement which resulted in free Europe's appeasement vis-à-vis Nazi territorial expansion, making the outbreak of war now look just a matter of time. Although Brecht was to keep returning to his play and modifying it for well-nigh two decades, the initial draft was completed swiftly. His *Arbeitsjournal* for 23 November 1938 records: 'DAS LEBEN DES GALILEI abgeschlossen, brauchte dazu drei Wochen' (*1*, p.35). Brecht had been toying with the material on and off for some years, certainly since the 300th anniversary of Galilei's recantation in 1933, which may explain the fact that he had little difficulty in producing an entire first draft during that November, the very month of the Nazis' ominous *Kristallnacht* pogrom.

The pre-war *Leben des Galilei* was unmistakably 'ein antinazistisches Stück' (*34*, p.273), illustrating the control a totalitarian system could exercise over individuals. Christian Møller, a Danish physicist Brecht consulted on scientific points, recalled: 'Brecht [interessierte] sich deshalb für Galilei, weil er eine Analogie zwischen der Inquisition und dem Nationalsozialismus in Deutschland sah' (*34*, p.115). Problematic vestiges of this original German focus are still in evidence in the play's final form. For instance, in the reference to 'ein tausendjähriges [...] Elend' (p.125), recalling Hitler's promise of a glorious 'Tausendjähriges Reich', or in Galilei's parting remark to Andrea at the end of Scene 14: 'Gib acht auf dich, wenn du durch Deutschland kommst, die Wahrheit unter dem Rock' (p.127). An abbreviated reference to the year '33' as the date of Galilei's recantation (p.123) similarly harks back to the original play's parallel between the events of 1633 and Hitler's 1933 *Machtergreifung*. More than one reading of these unexpurgated allusions is possible. One can lament the fact that Brecht had not yet ironed out all the discrepancies between his original Third Reich-oriented parable and its transformation in response to the nuclear bomb and that they remain as blemishes. A more charitable response is to assume that *Leben des Galilei* progressively becomes a parable facing in more than one direction and that specific pointers to *two* distinct spheres of reference, Nazi Germany and pre-Hiroshima America, are in varying degrees operative and jointly reinforce the sense of political urgency to the dangers outlined. It is, after all, in the nature of parables that they refuse to be tied down exclusively to one referential framework. Those exercized by the lack of fit between the play and one moment in history risk blurring the distinction between parable and systematic allegory.

At the outset, writing in Scandinavian exile, Brecht was understandably not keen to be over explicit about the Third Reich connotations of the work, fearing Danish reluctance to stage it if it was seen to be a hot potato (there was an injunction on exiles engaging in political activity). In a transparent attempt to put those hostile to his real concerns off the scent, he declared in an interview for the *Berlingske Tidende* of 6 January 1939 that the work had nothing to do with conditions in Hitler's Germany, but was purely a historical piece, set in seventeenth-century Italy where there was 'no Nazism and no fascism'. 'Conditions in those days', Brecht assured his Danish hosts, 'were completely different' (*45*, p.450). Notwithstanding Brecht's trenchant denials, parallels with contemporary Germany were at the very heart of the first version. Anyone, indeed, who believed Brecht capable of historical drama devoid of relevance to the contemporary world clearly could not have known him very well.

In its earliest form *Leben des Galilei* was not just concerned with the kind of deleterious suppression of truth that became the scourge of the Third Reich, with its ubiquitous use of fear as a method of political control. It also offered an example of the possibility of subversion; it is not merely chance that Galilei, towards the end of the play, carries on with his writing to produce the *Discorsi* which Andrea smuggles across the border. *He has become a resistance fighter during the course of the action.*

The pro-resistance slant of the original version comes across most explicitly in Scene 8. A figure (later removed) called 'der ältere Gelehrte' complains about the inhibiting climate of fear in Italy: 'Der Schaden des päpstlichen Dekrets, das den Kopernikus auf den Index gesetzt hat, ist riesig. Die Wissenschaften in den katholischen Ländern gehen zurück. Soll man wirklich schweigen?' (*BFA*5, p.72). Galilei's answer comes in the form of a fable:

> In die Wohnung des kretischen Philosophen Keunos, der wegen seiner freiheitlichen Gesinnung bei den Kretern sehr beliebt war, kam eines Tages während der Gewaltherrschaft ein gewisser Agent, der einen Schein vorzeigte, der von denen ausgestellt war, welche die Stadt beherrschten. Darauf stand, ihm sollte jede Wohnung gehören, in die er seinen Fuß setzte; ebenso sollte ihm auch jedes Essen gehören, das er verlange; ebenso sollte ihm auch jeder Mann dienen, den er sähe. Der Agent setzte sich auf einen Stuhl, verlangte Essen, wusch sich, legte sich nieder und fragte, mit dem Gesicht

zur Wand, vor dem Einschlafen: wirst du mir dienen? Keunos deckte ihn mit einer Decke zu, vertrieb die Fliegen, bewachte seinen Schlaf und wie an diesem Tage gehorchte er ihm sieben Jahre lang. Aber was immer er für ihn tat: vor einem hütete er sich wohl, das war: auch nur ein Wort zu sagen. Als nun die sieben Jahre um waren und der Agent dick geworden war vom vielen Essen, Schlafen und Befehlen, starb der Agent. Da wickelte ihn Keunos in die verdorbene Decke, schleppte ihn aus dem Haus, wusch das Lager, tünchte die Wände, atmete auf und antwortete: nein. (*BFA*5, pp.72f.)

Galilei's story is about biding one's time, not by sitting around and waiting for a change of regime, but by engaging in covert resistance. For Keunos's exaggerated hospitality – feeding and resting him to excess – has actually done the agent to death within the space of seven years. What looks like dumb obedience is really sabotage. This possibility is an uncomfortable one for Andrea: 'Mir gefällt diese Geschichte nicht, Herr Galilei' (*BFA*5, p.73). The astronomer's ex-pupil clings to a naive distinction between obeying the powers that be and wholeheartedly resisting them. Unable to understand the subtleties of more disguised forms of resistance, he resorts to an outdated moral yardstick, suspecting Keunos of being a shabby 'Mitläufer'. But Keunos's strategy is not to be judged on the basis of conventional morality. Despite appearances, he is not conniving with the enemy. What looks like collaboration eventually reveals itself as the approach of a fifth columnist. By the same token, in the original pre-war *Leben des Galilei*, the hero's recantation was to be understood as having bought him space to carry on with his work. In this first version, he is in regular contact with the underground movement of the time. Indeed, his sense of solidarity with local dissidents gives him the confidence to carry on with clandestine work on the *Discorsi*, although he still presents his actions in a self-deprecatory manner. On balance, the first version's concluding image of Galilei the resistance-fighter resembles the heroic figure that Andrea would have liked him to be, even in later rewritings of the play. As Andrea puts it in the final version, on hearing that the *Discorsi* have been completed and surreptitiously preserved despite the surveillance activities of the Church, 'Dies ändert alles. [...] Sie kamen zurück [...]. Sie gewannen die Muße, ein wissenschaftliches Werk zu schreiben, das nur Sie schreiben konnten' (pp.122f.). Yet in all versions but the first, Andrea's interpretation is shown to be wrong. There could eventually be no question of his having resorted to deliberate subterfuge for any heroic reason. Aware of his physical limits, Galilei recants out of naked fear:

> ANDREA So war es kein Plan?
> GALILEI Es war keiner. (p.123)

At least the initial version of the play had the agitational merit of dramatizing the possibility of covert resistance. This is what the exiled playwright still expected of the Germans trapped in his native country at the mercy of Hitler and his henchmen. Indeed, camouflaged resistance was also official Soviet policy at the time. The Seventh Congress of the Communist International in Moscow in 1935 heard Georgi Dimitrov recommend a 'Trojan Horse tactic' to those suffering under the yoke of Nazi oppression; behind a smokescreen of collaboration, resistance workers were to seek out opportunities for civil disobedience. That Dimitrov was the spokesman for such a strategy must have had a particular appeal in Brecht's eyes, for in a Nazi court a few years earlier the Bulgarian had specifically compared himself with Galilei before the Inquisition (a detail which may possibly have been the catalyst for Brecht's play).

Despite its dispiriting picture of the stranglehold of reactionary forces over Galilei's Italy and, by analogy, over twentieth-century Europe, the original version still managed to imply that covert acts of opposition were possible under totalitarianism. But when Brecht came back to the play some five years later in America, he could not conceal his dismay at just how little internal resistance there had been during the Third Reich. He was therefore loath to retain the *Widerstandskämpfer* aspect of his original hero.

Although the Galilei of the first version is presented exceptionally positively as a researcher who eventually becomes involved in resistance work, it would be wrong to assume that Brecht was simply targeting scientists or, for that matter, specifically the *Physikerzunft*. Granted, he did point to the crimes of concentration camp doctors and medical specialists involved in the Nazi euthanasia programme as supplying part of the ethical context to the play (*16*, pp.17ff.), but the abject capitulation of many Third Reich scientists was far from the sole butt of the work's criticism. *Leben des Galilei* can be more constructively approached as treating the scientist figure representatively, a reading corroborated by the majority of Brecht's early remarks about his play, which suggest that he is attacking the intelligentsia in general. A draft foreword refers to the dark days when Germany was witnessing 'eine beinahe totale Mobilmachung der Intelligenz' (*18*, p.59). 'Die Intelligenz sehen wir, ihr Wissen und ihr Gewissen verkaufen' (*34*, p.98). If Brecht could even suggest that 'Galilei markiert den Standard der italienischen Intellektuellen im ersten Drittel des 17. Jahrhunderts' (*18*, pp.71f), then presumably his counterparts in the Third Reich are also the intelligentsia *en masse*, not some narrower segment of society. According to one of Brecht's fellow exiles: 'Nie haben seine Freunde in den Entstehungsjahren [des Dramas] irgend etwas anderes gehört, als daß der *Galilei* [...] der deutsche Intellektuelle in den inneren und äußeren Entscheidungen genau jener Jahre [...] ist' (*58*, p.68).

Early on, Brecht entertained the idea of publishing his Galilei play alongside *Furcht und Elend des Dritten Reiches* ('Sie ergänzen sich', *2*, p.375). Such a plan reinforces the fact that the work began life as an analysis of the general intelligentsia's behaviour in the Third Reich rather than an exploration of the scientist's responsiblity under capitalism. *Furcht und Elend* does contain one scene, 'Deutsche Physik', in which two physicists are whispering in their laboratory about Einstein's theories, outlawed in Germany as 'Jewish Physics' and therefore taboo. This has led some commentators to conclude that the operative parallel is between the entire Galilei play and this one isolated episode. If, however, one bears in mind that a number of key episodes in *Furcht und Elend* treat intellectuals' betrayal of their ethical responsibilities (we encounter a judge, a police inspector, a doctor, a pastor, middle-class parents, as well as schoolteachers), then the two works have more in common than the 'Physikerdrama' reading allows. And as Livingstone has reminded us (*26*), the late thirties was the time when Brecht was working on his *Tui*-project, an exploration of intellectuals who sell out to capitalism – the 'Tuis', an abusive term derived from the inversion 'Tellekt-Ual-Ins', being a caricature of opportunist egg-heads who, by collaborating with regimes, legitimize them, instead of using their intelligence to take a stand against what is politically unacceptable.

Brecht's various references to 'die Intellektuellen' and 'die Intelligenz' give a clear indication of what Galilei is meant to represent, *not just in the first version of the play, but in all three versions*. Many features of the work are designed to bring out this general applicability. Indeed, it would be inconsistent for a man of Brecht's vision to single out physicists for an *ad hominem* attack. That such an over-specific reading has retained its popularity is perhaps an indication of just how comforting it is to see Brecht's play as being about *them* – about other people's betrayal of their responsibilities – rather than about the ethical shortcomings of wider groups in society.

The point at issue here is the relationship between the general and the particular. As Brecht puts it in his *Couragemodell 1949*, 'das Einzelne auffällig zu verknüpfen mit dem Allgemeinen, im großen Prozeß das Besondere festzuhalten, das ist die Kunst des Realisten' (*BFA*25, p.240). When Brecht, a realist on his own terms, writes elsewhere about 'Rundköpfe und Spitzköpfe', Salvation Army shenanigans, a courageous mother with a covered wagon, a chalk circle tug-of-love or even the occasional elephant, none but the obtusely literal-minded would fail to see beyond his vehicle for defamiliarizing and exploring an issue to what he is really writing about. Likewise, the scientist figure in *Leben des Galilei* deserves to be interpreted as a *representative element*, a functional ingredient in a parable with wider repercussions than the presentation material on the surface gives one grounds to expect. Thus, without wanting to deny the significance of the scientist figure in our century, I shall argue that there is substantial material – in all three versions of the play – to widen the thematic scope beyond the confines of any one profession's obligations to society, whether we are thinking of an American nuclear physicist or a German doctor. One unfortunate effect of Hiroshima has been an undue narrowing of Brecht's play, something which the intervening fifty years have done little to redress.

Some parts of *Leben des Galilei*, notably Scenes 13 and 14, do of course highlight the predicament of the scientist and the moral onus the figure bears: 'der Verfolg der Wissenschaft scheint [...] besondere Tapferkeit zu erheischen' (p.124). But the play's illustrations of what Schumacher calls 'negatives und positives Verhalten der Intellektuellen' (*34*, p.94) are by no means confined to scientist figures. To point to features which widen from the particular is not to jettison the generally accepted 'Physikerdrama' reading of *Leben des Galilei* lock, stock and barrel. That Galilei is a physicist and an astronomer remains a key aspect of the work's manifest content. Rather, it is to restore to its rightful place the skilful way in which Brecht locates this specific topical theme within a much larger framework of implications for society, thus deploying the scientist figure – here associated with the possibility of destruction – as a heightened illustration of problems encountered in the lives of virtually everyone suffering from that alienation which capitalism engenders.

One of the main aspects of *Leben des Galilei*, pointing in the direction of a wider (parabolic) reading of the material, is the way Galilei himself is presented. Many scenes present him as a paradigm of the kind of behaviour expected from all members of society, rather than as some sort of exceptional scientific genius. In Scene 3 he bears witness in characteristically crusading style to an unshakable belief in the power of reason. But it is the manner in which he nails his colours to the mast which is of interest here: 'Ich glaube an die sanfte Gewalt der Vernunft *über die Menschen*. Sie können ihr auf die Dauer nicht widerstehen [...]. Die Verführung, die von einem Beweis ausgeht, ist zu groß. [...] *Das Denken gehört zu den größten Vergnügungen der menschlichen Rasse*' (pp.34f., my emphasis). We are not being offered an image of any unique receptiveness to complicated experimental evidence. Instead the stress is on the power of reason which makes the scientist ideally a representative human being.

The idea that Galilei is no more than an enhanced version of those around him is brought out repeatedly. Seeking confirmation on a point of principle, he turns quite early on to his housekeeper for help: 'Frau Sarti, vielleicht können Sie [...] mir helfen. Sehen Sie, es ist eine Frage entstanden, über die wir uns nicht einig werden können, wahrscheinlich, weil wir zu viele Bücher gelesen haben. Es ist eine Frage über den Himmel, eine Frage die Gestirne betreffend. Sie lautet: ist es anzunehmen, daß das Große sich um das Kleine dreht, oder dreht wohl das Kleine sich um das Große?' Frau Sarti's down-to-earth reply ('Stelle ich Ihnen das Essen hin, oder stellen Sie es mir hin?') has Galilei enthusing to Sagredo: 'Und solche Leute sollen nicht die Wahrheit begreifen können? Sie schnappen danach!' (pp.35f.). Clearly, 'solche Leute', ordinary people exercising their common sense, are by no means on a different plane from Galilei. 'Vernunft' is virtually a synonym for common sense, rather than the preserve of rarified intellectuals.

The most significant of many features opening out *Leben des Galilei* beyond the confines of a 'Physikerdrama' is Andrea's heroism at the end of the play. Scene 15 is required as a counter-balance to Galilei's earlier capitulation. As a gesture of ethical commitment, it contributes to the play's uplifting ending. The work may begin with Galilei delivering a lesson in astronomy, but, more importantly, it concludes with Andrea giving his former mentor, and the audience, a lesson in social commitment. Andrea thereby becomes the much-needed *Widerstandskämpfer*, risking his life for the right cause in a manner which has little connexion with his scientific training and everything to do with his strong sense of obligation to society. Even in the final version, then, Brecht refuses to abandon the theme of resistance, he merely shows Galilei to be less exemplary than Andrea.

Andrea's concluding heroism is, in theory at least, a course of action available to anyone living under the yoke of oppression, be it

National Socialist, capitalist (or Stalinist). The stupidity of the border-guards, coupled with Andrea's feigned calmness at the checkpoint, runs the risk of underplaying the danger lurking just below the surface of Scene 15. Andrea is actually in great jeopardy, possibly more than he knows. But at least Galilei is aware of the odds: 'Solltest du erwägen, [die *Discorsi*] nach Holland mitzunehmen, würdest du natürlich die gesamte Verantwortung zu schultern haben' (p.122). The audience can appreciate, given the Inquisition's capabilities and those of its twentieth-century counterparts, just what it would mean for Andrea to be caught red-handed. Andrea's positive behaviour offsets Galilei's failure, just as mother and daughter are juxtaposed in *Mutter Courage und ihre Kinder*.

After this, the Galilei project was to become progressively more sceptical of people's ability to rise to the occasion.

Entitled simply *Galileo*, the second (English) version of the play, written in California between 1943 and 1947, was transformed by historical events from being an 'anti-Nazi Stück' into a very different kind of animal. Not just because, with the defeat of Hitler's Germany now virtually a foregone conclusion, Brecht was turning to other issues, but on account of one particular historical watershed in August 1945: 'Das "atomarische Zeitalter" machte sein Debüt in Hiroshima in der Mitte unserer Arbeit. Von heute auf morgen las sich die Biographie des Begründers der neuen Physik anders. Der infernalische Effekt der Großen Bombe stellte den Konflikt des Galilei mit der Obrigkeit seiner Zeit in ein neues, schärferes Licht' (*16*, p.10).

We must not, however, forget one Marxist factor which made the transformation of a play about the Third Reich into a comment on the post-Hiroshima world relatively easy, namely the doctrinaire interpretation of fascism which underpinned the first conception of the play. In *Fünf Schwierigkeiten beim Schreiben der Wahrheit* of 1938, Brecht rejects the view, prevalent in the West, that fascism represents 'eine neue dritte Macht neben (und über) Kapitalismus und Sozialismus'. According to the orthodox Socialist view: 'Der Faschismus ist eine historische Phase, in die der Kapitalismus eingetreten ist, insofern etwas Neues und zugleich Altes [...] *der Faschismus kann nur bekämpft werden als Kapitalismus, als nacktester, frechster, erdrückendster und betrügerischster Kapitalismus*' (*GW*18, pp.226f.). Brecht enquires: 'Wie will nun jemand die Wahrheit über den Faschismus sagen, gegen den er ist, wenn er nichts gegen den Kapitalismus sagen will, der ihn hervorbringt?' (*GW*18, p.227), a question which makes it clear that in his eyes any anti-fascist play worth its salt must at the same time take account of the capitalism-fascism relationship. This alignment of fascism with capitalism helps explain why even the first version of *Leben des Galilei*, highlighting the parallels between seventeenth-century Italy and Nazi Germany, could at the same time make Galilei's enemies in both the Church and the aristocracy look like prototypical capitalists. However one views this Marxist interpretation of National Socialism (and its detractors charge it with being too narrowly class-based), one should not underestimate the extent to which it colours the first version of the play, which, as Brecht remarked, 'zeigt, wie die Gesellschaft von ihren Individuen erpreßt, was sie von ihnen braucht' (*16*, p.13). As will become clear in the next chapter, the fact that, in order to survive, Galilei has to prostitute himself in various demeaning ways and abandon his values and eventually disown what he knows to be true because he can prove it to be so, illustrates what Marxism assumes capitalism does to people. Whenever Galilei withdraws into a specialization because he is unwilling to think beyond the end of his nose (e.g. the retreat to the flotation experiments when astronomy is becoming too dangerous, or his remark that he has written 'ein Buch über die Mechanik des Universums' and it is not his concern what ends it is put to (p.101)), we have illustrations of what Marx refers to as 'die knechtende Unterordnung der Individuen unter der Teilung der Arbeit' (*49*, p.291). This element, already unequivocally in evidence in the anti-Nazi first version, translates easily into the later indictment of · capitalism, above all American and West German capitalism, and its role in the use and proliferation of atomic weaponry. However, the Californian and (final) Berlin versions of Brecht's play do represent a much less contentious picture of the dark side of capitalism than his first version did of the nature of National Socialism.

In the aftermath of Hiroshima and Nagasaki, Galilei's role as 'sozialer Verbrecher' is brought out more emphatically. There are two substantial omissions which make for a marked difference between the original Danish version and the second Californian one. The plague scene, where Galilei risks his life to continue with his astronomical observations, is dropped, consequently the hero of *Galileo* becomes a noticeably less heroic figure. The final scene is also omitted, with the previous scene simply ending with a verse containing the lines: 'And, good folks, that was the end: / The Great Book over the border went' (*BFA5*, p.181), a rhyme which must have sounded purer to Brecht's ears than to Laughton's.

There are various respects in which the Danish version of the play and the subsequent (Californian and Berlin) ones differ. After the war comes a substantial reinterpretation of the central figure, in particular of his recantation (what was a clever subterfuge becomes abject surrender out of fear). In addition, the entire play is now related to the post-Hiroshima situation rather than Nazi Germany. This change of historical reference did not so much mark a watershed between the Danish and American versions, but was something that befell the American one while it was being written. Even in California, Brecht had initially set out to rewrite his play with a focus primarily on the oppressive atmosphere of Nazi Germany. Obviously, in the light of Hiroshima's impact – and Brecht's much-quoted preface to the American version, according to which 'die Atombombe ist sowohl als technisches als auch soziales Phänomen das klassische Endprodukt seiner [Galileis] wissenschaftlichen Leistung und seines sozialen Versagens' (*16*, p.13) – *Leben des Galilei* has come to be seen as a play about the particular responsibilities of the scientist. However, as we have seen, an unfortunate by-product of the play's metamorphosis was the way in which a most un-Brechtian ossification to the work's reception set in, narrowing its import unduly to a less representative parable than it was in the 1938 version and fixing it in time as if it were forever tied to the events of 1945. Now that all three versions of the work are accessible in the new critical edition, we have the evidence upon which to decide whether we are dealing with three fundamentally dissimilar plays or merely local variations on one single work that can be read against different historical backcloths.

The Cold War of the late forties and 1950s encouraged a further reading of *Galileo/Leben des Galilei*, one which had understandable attractions, even though it was probably not part of Brecht's main intention. If an analogy could be drawn between the repressiveness of Galilei's Italy and the *Gleichschaltung* of Nazi Germany or capitalist America, one could also be posited with conditions in the Stalinist USSR and its East European satellites. When he came to work up the third version of the play in the 1950s, Brecht may have drawn on his personal experiences at the hands of McCarthyite America in his depiction of the Inquisition's methods of thought control; he may also, the argument runs, have borne in mind the thought-control techniques employed by the communists. When Hannah Arendt saw the American version in 1947, she observed that the play '[paßt] mit gleicher Genauigkeit auf die Nazi-Diktatur wie auf die bolschewistische Diktatur' (*4*, p.56). Isaac Deutscher was later to note in his Trotsky biography that the play, originally written 'at the height of the Great Purges', summed up the ideological predicament of 'the capitulators in Russia'. Claiming that 'it was through the prism of the Bolshevik experience that [Brecht] saw Galileo going down on his knees before the Inquisition [...]. Galileo is Zinoviev, or Bukharin or Rakovsky in historical costume', Deutscher goes on to suggest that the work 'epitomizes [...] the problem of Trotsky and Stalinist Russia rather than Galileo's quandary in Renaissance Italy' (*46*, p.370). Relating the machinations of Church and Inquisition in the play to the repressive OGPU/NKVD and the 'show trials' of Bukharin, Zinoviev and Rakovsky in late 1930s Russia is a reading that has found renewed support in various quarters over the years. An extreme form of the argument that *Leben des Galilei* reflects left rather than right-wing political oppression comes with Betty Nance Weber's attempt at showing, often through contrived detailed analogies, that Brecht's play 'chronicled Soviet history from 1917 to 1938' (*38*, p.64). Weber reads *Leben des Galilei* as a *Schlüsseldrama*, the historical characters and situations of which equate with events in the Soviet Union during the 1930s. There is also a biographical variant to this interpretation of the play as a parable about the excesses of Stalinism: one which sees the work chronicling Brecht's own predicament, the focus being less on the Moscow 'show trials' than on the author's vexed relationship with the iron-fisted establishment in the GDR. The life and lies of Galileo Galilei are then read as a mirror of the various problems Brecht himself experienced with a Stalinist regime, the ideology of which he shared, but the methods of which he tacitly rejected.

The East German critic Ernst Schumacher was one of the first from behind the Iron Curtain to risk speculation about the potential relationship of *Leben des Galilei* to the Moscow trials. He came to the guarded conclusion that these events had at most a technical influence on the way Brecht shaped the grand act of self-indictment by his hero in Scene 14. According to Schumacher, it would be over simplistic to equate the Inquisition here with Stalin's purge machinery. The influence of the 'show trials' and the whole atmosphere of that dark time lies 'lediglich im Formalen' (*34*, p.112); i.e. Bukharin's self-criticism at his trial gave the playwright the 'solution' to the problem of how to allow his hero to err and yet ensure that his audience saw the true issues (a problem also experienced in the case of Mutter Courage). As an orthodox pre-'Thaw' GDR critic, Schumacher was clearly obliged to reject any fundamental analogy between the reactionary Italy of the play and the Soviet Union or the Eastern bloc. Nevertheless, the parallel still continues to prove attractive, even to post-Cold-War critics. Only recently, Werner Zimmermann reiterated the claim 'daß gleichermaßen die Verfolgungen der Intellektuellen im Deutschland Hitlers wie in der Sowjetunion Stalins als Anlaß und Modell für die Konzeption der ersten Fassung gelten können' (*43*, p.28). In principle, at least, this would seem to be a viable standpoint, given that parables are usually of such a high level of abstraction that they can apply to a number of situations. Indeed, Brecht did once describe the Church in this play as an 'Obrigkeit [...] im Grund austauschbar mit mancher anderen' (*16*, p.10). Nevertheless, as we shall discover, this particular 'Obrigkeit' is depicted as quintessentially capitalist, something which could hardly be claimed of that in Stalin's USSR. Consequently, a reading that equates the oligarchy oppressing Galilei with the Stalinist brand of communism has to turn a blind eye to many of the particulars in Brecht's play.

The third version of *Leben des Galilei* (the so-called 'Berliner Fassung'), the one on which the following study will concentrate, was for a long time the only one in print. It was completed in 1956, yet only staged posthumously by the Berliner Ensemble in January of the following year, although its *Uraufführung* by the Kölner Kammerspiele had taken place some months earlier. Given the Cold War atmosphere of the period, this possibly surprising premiere in the West can be explained by the fact that Brecht died in August 1956 whilst still in the process of putting the final touches to a London guest performance by his Ensemble. The East Berlin production, with Ernst Busch in the title-role, had to be taken over by Erich Engel. All this caused delays in Berlin and allowed a West German production to pip the Ensemble at the post, in fact an auspicious event because it broke the Federal Republic's embargo on Brecht's work since the June uprising of 1953.

The existence of three versions of the play, extending over more than a decade and a half, may seem odd, when one recalls how early Brecht had voiced misgivings about its quality. His *Arbeitsjournal* for 25 February 1939 calls the work 'technisch ein großer rückschritt, [...] allzu opportunistisch', adding: 'man müßte das stück vollständig neu schreiben, wenn man diese "brise, die von neuen küsten kommt", diese rosige morgenröte der wissenschaft, haben will. alles mehr direkt, ohne die interieurs, die "atmosphäre", die einfühlung. und alles auf planetarische demonstrationen gestellt' (*1*, p.32). Brecht did, of course, come back to the work; but as he noted after Hiroshima, 'wir hatten nur wenige Änderungen zu machen, keine einzige in der Struktur' (*16*, p.10), which, while not being strictly true, nevertheless suggests that he did not rethink the play radically enough to take account of his original doubts. Schumacher argues that he was too harsh with himself and that the play was both less 'opportunistisch', i.e. accommodated to the tastes of American audiences, and more profoundly dialectical and experimental than his recriminations would suggest – an assessment which the following analysis will largely reinforce.

Why then did Brecht return to his play in the mid-fifties, after almost a decade, if not to embark on substantial improvements? Schumacher assumes that the dangers posed by West German remilitarization and a new threat from the hydrogen bomb (what he, not Brecht, calls 'der "zweite Sündenfall" der Kernphysiker', *34*, p.242) supplied the main impetus for the work's revival. Brecht's intense interest at this time in the trial of J. Robert Oppenheimer for refusing to participate in the H-bomb's development is well attested and was no doubt a factor, as was the fact that he was also toying with the possibility of a play about Einstein. It may not be by chance that it was 1953, the year of the Berlin uprising, when Brecht first proposed the idea of a new version of the play to his then collaborators, Ruth Berlau, Elisabeth Hauptmann and Benno Besson. But even if the events of the June uprising did stimulate him to rethink the material, their impact can be read in divergent ways. For a socialist, the Berlin *Aufstand* could be seen as the West's meddling in internal GDR affairs, not just as another instance of the dead hand of the Stalinist police state. And in any case, if Brecht was frequently critical of the regime under which he had chosen to end his days, he still remained more disturbed by expanding Western militarism than by bungled communism. In his eyes, the country which had been the first to release the A-bomb on a civilian population could just as well be the first to drop the H-bomb.

No matter what combination of motives sent Brecht back to the drawing-board, the fact remains that the final Berlin version is the most inclusive of all three. Back in now come the plague episode and Andrea's taking the *Discorsi* across the border. Galilei's self-indictment in Scene 14 becomes the most probing and powerfully formulated in any of the three versions. A number of further details which we shall be considering in subsequent chapters were only added at this late stage. But although we think of this 'Berliner Fassung' as Brecht's, it was, like each previous one, a collective enterprise. In the same way as Charles Laughton, Hanns Eisler and

Margarete Steffin, among others, had made a considerable input into the earlier versions, so here too we are dealing with the product of an Ensemble consisting of more than just actors and playwright. Just as Galilei's scientific discoveries are presented as being the result of team-work, so too Brecht's third and final attempt at interpreting the life of Galileo Galilei owed substantial debts to a whole host of helpers and collaborators.

2. Galilei's Behaviour: The Anatomy of a Betrayal

Leben des Galilei shadows its protagonist for more than a quarter of a century, starting with a period of personal frustration in 1609 ('bin 46 Jahre alt und habe nichts geleistet, was mich befriedigt', p.20) to just after 1636, when his *Discorsi* cross the border to the outside world. During this time, Galilei consistently towers above the other characters. Scene 13's rejection of the idea 'daß große und kleine Maschinen gleich ausdauernd seien' (p.114) leaves us in no doubt that Galilei is a 'große Maschine' whose stature is more than a matter of mere body size. Brecht sometimes referred to his project as '*Das* Leben des Galilei', but in the end dropped the definite article, partly to echo the seventeenth-century title-formula *Leben und Taten des...*, but also to shift the emphasis from surface biography to his figure's liveliness. Galilei is nothing if not physically and intellectually lively: 'ein Phänomen wie etwa Richard III', characterized above all by 'Vitalität' (*16*, p.47).

Since the play begins with Galilei's dissatisfaction at his paltry achievements and ends with his *magnum opus* wending its way to a Dutch publisher, we might seem to be dealing with a success story: the rise and triumph of a great scientist despite all obstacles. But the picture is more complex than this. We witness a number of high and low points to the hero's fortunes. That part of Scene 1 where we hear him singing the praises of a new era of discovery, invention and social enlightenment finds him at his ethical and political peak, even though he may appear to be treading water intellectually (and has to, if he is to come across as the victim of an exploitative system). This marks the pinnacle from which Galilei is soon to slip, although the audience is at first likely to see him as a totally positive figure. We hear him taking stock of recent scientific advances, buoyant at science's ability to improve the working conditions and welfare of the common people. What is more, he is of a piece with what he is saying. With his dynamic presence, he palpably embodies the New Age, rather than merely extolling it. He takes enormous pleasure in his appetites and physicality, he relishes his own powers of rhetoric and savours the poetry of others; and he rejoices in life: not just a narrow scientist, in other words, but more an *uomo universale* in the Renaissance tradition. Brecht's description of him (in a letter to the artist Hans Tombrock in March 1941) as 'ein kräftiger Physiker mit embonpoint, Sokrates-Gesicht, ein lärmender, vollsaftiger Mann mit Humor, der neue Physikertyp, irdisch, ein großer Lehrer. Lieblingshaltung: Bauch vorgestreckt, beide Hände auf den beiden Arschbacken' (*16*, p.27) well captures the vitality, charisma and infectious *joie de vivre* of the figure we encounter at the outset.

Significantly, Galilei's initial role is that of teacher: Brecht intended a contrast between 'die Lust am Produzieren und das Vermitteln von Wissen', displayed during Galilei's finer moments, and 'die kapitalistische Entmenschlichung der "Ware Arbeitskraft"' (*16*, p.31), in the more compromising ones to follow. Sadly, the more illustrious Galilei becomes as a scientist, the more the rest of the man shrinks to the stature of those 'erfinderische Zwerge, die für alles gemietet werden können' (p.126). He progressively betrays the principles paraded in Scene 1 and ends up 'ein Verbrecher' (p.81) – not in any legal sense, but from the point of view of the modern, politically aware audience. His 'Verbrechen' was intended to epitomize 'die "Erbsünde" der modernen Naturwissenschaften', a complex charge which for Brecht is bound up with what is diagnosed as immoral, ostrich-like specialization.

> Aus der neuen Astronomie, die eine neue Klasse, das Bürgertum, zutiefst interessierte, da sie den revolutionären sozialen Strömungen der Zeit Vorschub leistete, machte er eine scharf begrenzte Spezialwissenschaft. [...] Die Atombombe ist sowohl als technisches als auch soziales Phänomen das klassische Endprodukt [...] seines sozialen Versagens. (*16*, pp.12f)

Or, in the words of Galilei's confession: 'ich überlieferte mein Wissen den Machthabern, es zu gebrauchen, es nicht zu gebrauchen, es zu mißbrauchen, ganz, wie es ihren Zwecken diente' (p.126). In fact, we witness relatively little abuse of Galilei's findings by the state, for *Leben des Galilei* (no doubt by virtue of the fact that it originally reflected conditions in the Third Reich) is more concerned with the suppression of findings than their appropriation and exploitation. By and large, the play concentrates on two further, but related themes: Galilei's reluctance to display adequate social commitment at various stages of his life and a powerful establishment's ability to suppress unwelcome knowledge and intimidate people, even to the point of forcing them to deny demonstrable truths. It is not hard to see that the target of all this is less the power structure of the time, or even one particular Italian astronomer, than twentieth-century 'Verbrecher' and their accomplices.

The play not only dissects Galilei's story with our own century's problems in mind, it even uses a behavioural model which is only at a writer's disposal in the present age. For, as Brecht stressed, his work 'bricht weitgehend mit der Gewohnheit des üblichen Theaters, aus den Charakteren die Handlungen zu begründen, die Handlungen dadurch der Kritik zu entziehen, daß sie als aus den Charakteren, die sie vollziehen, unhinderbar, mit Naturgesetzlichkeit hervorgehend dargestellt werden' (*GW*16, p.551). If non-Brechtian drama usually interprets people's misbehaviour as a consequence of character defects, then a certain fatalism is likely to be the end result. Audiences assume that because the figures on stage are what they are, they cannot help doing what they do. An extreme version of this is the association of a pattern of inevitable events (seen as Fate) with the tragic flaw in the protagonist's character (*hamartia*, as Aristotle's *Poetics* calls it). To combat any such paralysing fatalism, *Leben des Galilei* shifts attention from individual psychology towards socio-economics, thus pinpointing the conditioning leading to given behaviour patterns. This new emphasis may explain why Brecht welcomed Charles Laughton's reluctance 'im Psychischen herumzukramen' (*GW*17, p.1120). According to Käthe Rülicke: Brecht 'sprach [...] auf den Proben fast nie über den

Charakter einer Figur, sondern über ihre Art, sich zu verhalten; er sagte beinahe nie, was ein Mensch *ist*, sondern was er *tut*' (*16*, p.107). He even went so far as to declare: 'Man sollte niemals vom Charakter einer Figur ausgehen, denn der Mensch hat keinen Charakter' (*17*, p.72). Whether he fully subscribed to such an extreme standpoint or whether this was merely a provocational strategy is difficult to decide. There are undoubted attractions for a Marxist in stressing social conditioning and playing down (or even rejecting) the conventional notion of character. In the words of *Die Dreigroschenoper*, 'Wir wären gut – anstatt so roh / Doch die Verhältnisse, sie sind nicht so' (*GW*2, p.2). In other words, if one starts out with the assumption that capitalism forces people to behave in a dog-eat-dog way, then it is possible to live more comfortably with the hypothesis that a change of political system will be conducive to improved behaviour. Character orientation thus becomes associated with inexorable tragedy, whereas a focus on socially conditioned behaviour is more likely to imply the feasibility of change. As Brecht says of Mutter Courage, she embodies, as mother and profiteer, an 'entsetzlicher Widerspruch [...], der [sie] vernichtete, ein Widerspruch, der gelöst werden konnte, aber nur von der Gesellschaft selbst und in langen, schrecklichen Kämpfen' (*GW*16, p.896). Within such an ideological matrix, the ultimate solution to anti-social conduct must be seen to lie in a changed society, not merely in the reform (or elimination) of the individual. This is where Galilei's self-criticism in Scene 14 gives only a part of the story. He blames himself exclusively for his failures, whereas Brecht's play has by then demonstrated the extent to which they stem from outside conditions.

Brecht talked of his Galilei as a kind of Humpty-Dumpty figure who also 'had a great fall' and whom 'all the King's horses and all the King's men' couldn't 'put [...] together again' (*16*, p.152). However, the analogy is, at best, question-begging. Galilei did not simply fall, he was pushed – by the near-feudal conditions under which he had to live. And he didn't so much suddenly fall off a wall as gradually slide down a slippery slope; hence Brecht's question '*Wann wird Galilei zum Schädling?*' (*16*, p.63) is not an easy one to answer. The other image the author often applied to his protagonist also stands in need of modification, namely that of Adam falling from grace, Galilei's final recantation as 'die "Erbsünde" der modernen Naturwissenschaften', the 'Sündenfall[s] der bürgerlichen Wissenschaften am Beginn ihres Aufstiegs' (*16*, pp.12, 76). For the story is more one of conditioning coupled with coercion than any simple temptation to surrender to blandishments. Many episodes show the extent to which the hero's ultimate betrayal and his various other (earlier) negative acts are largely conditioned by their social context. This tallies with Brecht's intention to make the underlying patterns of 'Ursache' and 'Wirkung' clearly visible in his theatre (*GW*16, pp.524, 576). What he, as a Marxist, took to be such laws of cause and effect – essentially political and economic pressures acting on individuals and making them behave in certain ways detrimental to their class interests – was what had to be placed in the foreground (*GW*16, pp.546, 654, 656).

One of the earliest examples of this pattern lies in the relationship between Scenes 1 and 2. In Scene 1's encounter between Galilei and Herr Priuli, the 'Kurator' of the University of Padua, who visits Galilei and refuses his request for a salary rise, fobbing him off with the claim that the values of the Republic of Venice are those of the free market, Galilei is given to understand that the academic world is governed unashamedly by business criteria. Knowledge is just another commodity and an academic is someone with knowledge to sell. 'Sie können für das Wissen, das Sie verkaufen, nur so viel verlangen, als es dem, der es Ihnen abkauft, einbringt. [...] Verachten Sie nicht den Handel, Herr Galilei' (pp.18f.). However, things are not as straightforward as this makes them seem. For Venice, expediently capitalizing on its reputation as 'die Republik [...], in der die Inquisition nichts zu sagen hat' (p.17), is able to acquire academics at well below their outside market price and exploit them, not only by paying a pittance but by rewarding them grudgingly according to an ingenious selective principle which favours money-spinning results: 'Skudi wert ist nur, was Skudi bringt' (p.18). When Galilei objects to being underpaid ('Euer Schutz der Gedankenfreiheit ist ein ganz gutes Geschäft, wie? [...] freier Handel, freie Forschung. Freier

Handel mit der Forschung, wie?' p.18), he is told to go off and make a lucrative discovery. As Brecht noted in a draft introduction: 'das Werk zeigt, wie die Gesellschaft von ihren Individuen erpreßt, was sie von ihnen braucht' (*16*, p.13). Needless to say, offering people inducements to behave as the state requires is also a form of 'Erpressung'.

This episode, an invention on Brecht's part (the real Galilei enjoyed adequate remuneration), supplies the causal nexus for the handing over of the pirated telescope. If society chooses to live by a Thatcherite set of values, with science reduced to the role of a slave to state interests, then Galilei assumes this gives him licence to deceive his masters. At the start of Scene 2 he clearly feels no qualms about lying through his teeth to the assembled Venetian dignitaries and palming off what he calls his 'vollkommen neues Instrument' as the 'Frucht siebenzehnjähriger geduldiger Forschung' (p.23). His appropriation of the telescope idea is a tactic to buy himself intellectual breathing space. What we are confronted with here is not so much an inveterate liar or purloiner of intellectual property as someone whose actions are shown to result from the way he has been maltreated. That the mercenary Venetian authorities receive their comeuppance by being cheated in this fashion (a fact which will soon emerge as the compromising boatload of telescopes arrives from Holland), simply adds further piquancy to the second scene of the play. Even if Galilei had not been 'found out' by the Venetian authorities, one suspects he would eventually have become unable to carry on working under such adverse conditions, not least because he has a certain minimum expectation of the good life ('ich will die Fleischtöpfe' (p.37)).

As a direct result of the financial and psychological pressures we observe in the early episodes, Scene 4 begins with a heading informing the audience 'GALILEI HAT DIE REPUBLIK VENEDIG MIT DEM FLORENTINER HOF VERTAUSCHT' (p.40). The formulation is revealing. That someone should abandon the safe haven of a republic for some quasi-feudal courtly world is a miscalculation. Just what price such a change of domicile will exact can already be gauged from the fawning terms of Galilei's letter, quoted at the end of the previous scene. To have to conclude his approach to the boy-prince with 'Sehne ich mich doch nach nichts so sehr, als Euch näher zu sein, der aufgehenden Sonne, welche dieses Zeitalter erhellen wird' (p.39) hardly squares with the breezy disrespect for authority flaunted in Scene 1, and even has Galilei metaphorically referring to the static sun as 'aufgehend'. The man of principle is already becoming, in small ways, a 'Verbrecher' according to his own later pronouncement ('wer sie [die Wahrheit] weiß und sie eine Lüge nennt, der ist ein Verbrecher!' p.81). That the scene title expresses Galilei's move with the verb 'vertauschen', the vocabulary of exchange and commerce (if not self-deception), draws attention to the dangerous course now being embarked upon. Galilei is moving from a state which offers protection to its scholars, albeit while paying them a pittance, to one where he will be offered substantial rewards ('die Fleischtöpfe', time for research, fame at court), but by doing so he will effectively come within the reach of the Inquisition. It is something he would not have contemplated, if economic circumstances had not become so intolerable.

The hand of social causality lies behind not only major developments like Galilei's move to Florence, but even local details. When Andrea is informed in Scene 1 that the appearance of a well-heeled prospective pupil, Ludovico Marsili, is going to have repercussions for their early-morning routine – 'Es wird auf deine Kosten gehen, Andrea. Du fällst natürlich dann aus. [...] du zahlst nichts' (p.15) – attention is drawn to the circumstances under which such a shabby remark becomes possible. It is only in a world dominated by the quasi-capitalist ethos of the Venetian Republic that Galilei's 'natürlich' makes sense. It would be wrong to be seduced by the Humpty Dumpty and 'Erbsünde' metaphors into assuming that Galilei engages in only one grand act of betrayal. In small ways he over and over again prepares the ground for his ultimate climb-down, which makes good sense, for if the behaviour under inspection is by and large socially determined, it would be illogical to expect just one unique 'Verbrechen'. We are presented with a plethora of mini-betrayals and compromises as the play proceeds.

Brecht, in any case, once declared that the real betrayal comes, not with Galilei's recantation, but earlier on in Scene 11: 'Der Stückeschreiber zieht es vor, den *Widerruf* des Galilei hier zu plazieren, anstatt denselben vor der Inquisition stattfinden zu lassen' (*16*, p.67). So, apart from minor acts of surrender running through much of the play, we have two main candidates for the accolade of supreme betrayal: the capitulation before the Inquisition in Scene 13 and Galilei's self-isolation at a point in Scene 11.

This scene has Vanni, the owner of an iron foundry, coming to Galilei with the offer of an historically momentous alliance: 'ich möchte die Gelegenheit benützen, Ihnen zu versichern, daß wir von der Manufaktur auf Ihrer Seite sind. [...] Hinter Ihnen stehen die oberitalienischen Städte, Herr Galilei' (pp.100f.). What is being extended is the hand of the newly emerging progressive forces: 'das Angebot der fortschrittlichen bürgerlichen Klasse' (*16*, p.67). That a Marxist writer should see such a gesture as a golden opportunity is logical. This was the most promising new power base of the time. (By contrast, it would have been an anachronism to make too much of a potential alliance between Galilei and the proletariat.) Indeed, there may also be a more specific allusion here, dating from the 1930s, when the idea of a 'Volksfront' against fascism, uniting Marxists with a motley crew of socialist and liberal factions, was being recommended by the Party. Brecht's idea that failure to seize this opportunity is the biggest mistake in the entire play makes good sense in contemporary political terms. Rejecting an alliance with what are currently, *faute de mieux*, the progressive forces of history, whatever their complexion, is a more far-reaching political crime than recanting under duress at the hands of one's ideological enemies.

Even Vanni's brushoff is socially determined, for it has to be understood in the light of the carnival scene which has just shown how politically threatening certain interpretations of Galilei's ideas are now becoming among the people. Sensing dangerous repercussions, Galilei is withdrawing, snail-like, into his specialization, just at the time when the Church is beginning to sense just what political dynamite his discoveries are. He thus rebuffs Vanni, selfishly stressing his own weaknesses ('Ich kann mich nicht als Flüchtling sehen. Ich schätze meine Bequemlichkeit'), and even tries to convince himself of the insignificance of Vanni's offer ('Ich kenne Macht von Ohnmacht auseinander', p.101), which of course he seldom does. Revealingly it is only when he is back with Virginia that Galilei ventures his most shameful remark (as if lacking the courage to say it to Vanni's face): 'Jeder Nächstbeste mit irgendeiner Beschwerde hierzulande wählt mich als seinen Wortführer, besonders an Orten, wo es mir nicht gerade nützt. Ich habe ein Buch geschrieben über die Mechanik des Universums, das ist alles. Was daraus gemacht oder nicht gemacht wird, geht mich nichts an' (p.101).

Brecht himself has furnished the best gloss to this in one of his notes to *Leben des Galilei*:

> Die Bourgeoisie isoliert im Bewußtsein des Wissenschaftlers die Wissenschaft, stellt sie als autarke Insel hin, um sie praktisch mit *ihrer* Politik, *ihrer* Wirtschaft, *ihrer* Ideologie verflechten zu können. Das Ziel des Forschers ist 'reine' Forschung, das Produkt der Forschung ist weniger rein. Die Formel $E = mc^2$ ist ewig gedacht, an nichts gebunden. So können andere die Bindungen vornehmen: die Stadt Hiroshima ist plötzlich sehr kurzlebig geworden. Die Wissenschaftler nehmen für sich in Anspruch die Unverantwortlichkeit der Maschinen. (*16*, p.16)

In other words, when scientists skulk behind the comforting notion of pure science and trying to salve their consciences, they play right into the hands of governments waiting to appropriate their discoveries. Instead of being autonomous ('autark'), science remains effectively embedded in a political matrix. Yet Brecht sees it as in capitalism's interest to ensure that individual researchers do not perceive this, just as it is convenient for scientists to develop a form of tunnel vision which blocks out the implications of their findings for society at large. Such cultivated myopia, the retreat into specialization which makes people putty in the hands of the powers that be, is intended as a further illustration of the way capitalism engenders a widespread condition of alienation ('Entfremdung').

So far we have been looking at aspects of Galilei's behaviour as a scientist within the context of the state(s) in which he lives and works. But Brecht's protagonist also has a private life, and this too contributes to the political picture of his conditioning.

Galilei uses people at a number of points in the play: Andrea is frequently required to run errands beyond the call of duty; during the plague Galilei expects people to risk infection supplying him with books; and in various scenes we witness him using fellow enthusiasts as unpaid labour. However, his treatment of Virginia is one of the most opportunistic features of his private life. Keith Dickson has objected that 'Brecht played his meanest trick on his historical model by falsifying his private life as well, in order to make him more negative as a human being and thus elicit a more critical response from the audience' (*8*, p.93). The aspect of Galilei's behaviour in question is his treatment of his daughter. Indeed, one of the play's main question-begging antitheses is that between Galilei's paternal attitude to the young Andrea and the way he maltreats Virginia.

In contrast to this unattractive aspect of the stage character's private life, the real historical Galilei had three children (all illegitimate), the second of whom, named Virginia, entered a convent. But there is no evidence of any bad blood between either her or the other two children and their father, who was tireless in his financial support of them and a number of other dependants. Brecht's Galilei, on the other hand, has but one child whom he treats callously throughout virtually the entire play.

As early as Scene 2 Virginia can be seen being exploited by her father, albeit in a relatively minor way. As part of the pageant laid on to hand over Galilei's telescope to the dignitaries of the Venetian Republic, poor Virginia, with her small walk-on role, seems as much part of the trimmings as the new 'Lederfutteral' and the velvet cushion on which the instrument is displayed. Galilei is already in a sense prostituting his daughter, just as he is taking the first steps towards prostituting his own integrity. (*'Galilei erkauft seinen Komfort mit Handlangerdiensten, er prostituiert seinen*

Intellekt', *16*, p.117.) When the fourteen-year-old Virginia asks him in the next scene (where the true powers of the telescope are starting to emerge) 'Darf ich durchschauen?', all he can come up with is 'Warum? [...] Es ist kein Spielzeug' (p.36). And later when, feigning interest in his work, she inquires whether he has made any new discoveries since he has had it, the only response she gets is a terse 'Nichts für dich' (p.36). All this stands in marked contrast to the eagerness to teach Andrea, Federzoni or the Little Monk.

The depths of Galilei's callousness come in Scene 9, where his renewed astronomical investigations and his abrasive treatment of Ludovico, now Virginia's intended, cause the nobleman to leave in a huff, thus putting a stop to any hope of marriage between them. The splendid dramatic curtain to this scene has a proud Virginia excitedly coming on stage in her 'Brautkleid', only to discover that Ludovico has left her in the lurch. Uttering the words 'Du hast ihn weggeschickt, Vater', she faints. His response, which is more an aside to himself than a reply, is 'Ich muß es wissen' (p.93). Not only are his experiments of the moment more important to him than his own daughter's marital prospects, he also betrays a gross lack of concern for Virginia's devastated emotional predicament.

Nevertheless, Galilei's 'auf dem Glück [seiner] Tochter Herumtrampeln mit [seinen] großen Füßen', as Frau Sarti calls it (p.90), may have another side to it. We need to bear in mind that in the course of the play Virginia becomes a 'Spitzel der Inquisition' (*16*, p.69), a fifth columnist working for Rome. At this late point, where Virginia is an agent for Galilei's ideological enemies, his behaviour towards her might seem to have a certain justification to it: he is treating her (correctly, from a Marxist standpoint) as his class enemy.

In Scene 4, the young Grand Duke Cosmo picks up one of the astronomical models and puts it on his lap. Andrea, seeing this, turns on him with the telling words 'Du sollst es hergeben. Das ist kein Spielzeug für Jungens' (p.42). On one level this is one of those remarks (cf. 'Hier geht es zu wie in einem Taubenschlag', pp.14, 41) which reveal how fond the young Andrea is of imitating Galilei. But both phrases are used when class enemies appear. The 'Taubenschlag' simile was first heard when Ludovico arrived on the scene, now it is used to make Cosmo feel in the way; and if the 'kein Spielzeug' rebuff is largely because Cosmo is a member of the nobility, then it is conceivably being directed in a similar spirit at Virginia as a class enemy.

Brecht repeatedly cautioned against the dangers of misplaced emotion, not least when rational judgments become clouded by blood ties (witness *Mutter Courage und ihre Kinder* and *Der kaukasische Kreidekreis*). To dismiss the father's hostile treatment of Virginia as an author's 'meanest trick' or to object to Galilei's callousness could be to miss the political point Brecht is trying to make. Yet even if one does concede a certain ideological rationale to Galilei's behaviour, this may still remain an uncomfortable insight. What is in theory politically correct may yet come across as reprehensible. Why does Galilei not make an attempt to change his daughter, especially given that he himself bears much responsibility for the way she is? After all, he drove her into the arms of the Church, with the Inquisitor becoming a father substitute, just as Frau Sarti had to be a mother substitute earlier on. It is not as if Galilei did not spend time and energy trying to change the attitudes of others; so why does he give up so soon in the case of his daughter? (Presumably, not just because he is a male chauvinist like his creator.) It may be too convenient to agree with Käthe Rülicke that 'Galileis Verhalten [kann] nicht als Frage seines Charakters, sondern als gesellschaftliche Notwendigkeit gezeigt werden' (*16*, p.112). For the economic pressures that can make a Galilei give up teaching Andrea in favour of Ludovico do not prevent him from treating the boy and his lab assistants with common humanity. Galilei's relationship to Virginia remains one of the more intractable aspects of the figure's presentation. Given that it is only in the final of the three versions that the treatment of Virginia is presented so negatively, it is possible to see this inserted feature as a deliberate response on Brecht's part to the challenge of making Galilei both a 'Held' and a 'Verbrecher' (cf. *16*, p.123), but in political rather than character-based moral terms.

Such examples of 'unheroic' behaviour on Galilei's part as have been examined so far (and there are others) might be thought of as amounting to cumulative evidence against him. The case against Galilei rests not just on the fact that he is the man who capitulated to the 'Obrigkeit' of the time by denying the truths he had discovered; it is vital that we associate him with many other peccadillos and misdemeanours. In fact, one can detect a distinct pattern to the evidence marshalled against him: minor examples of prostitution of his intellect and the exploitation of others in the early scenes of the play gradually give way to grosser forms of abuse (in the case of Virginia) and historically more momentous betrayals (Vanni, the recantation). But superimposed on this one pattern of a gradual worsening of conduct motivated by the increasing political and economic pressures on him, first in the Venetian Republic and later in Florence and Rome, there is another pattern: that of contradictory behaviour at virtually all stages of his life. For Galilei is the man who can say to Andrea in Scene 1 'Ich will gerade, daß auch du es begreifst' (p.11) and yet resolve to discontinue the boy's early-morning tuition when Ludovico turns up radiating the aura of a student who pays well. This is the scientist who can say 'wer sie [die Wahrheit] weiß und sie eine Lüge nennt, der ist ein Verbrecher!' (p.81) and yet do that very thing, if not in the case of Vanni's proposal, then certainly before the Inquisition. This is the socially enlightened man who can lay claim to a passionate concern for the predicament of Campagna peasants in his discussion with the Little Monk and place such weight on disputing in the vernacular so that his lens-grinder Federzoni can understand the debate, and yet betray this very class of people in both his surrender to the demands of the 'Machthaber' and in his blindness to the wider context of his work ('Was daraus gemacht oder nicht gemacht wird, geht mich nichts an', p.101). As this pattern suggests, contradiction as a principle may be one of the main avenues to an understanding of Brecht's protagonist.

In the first of his 'Nachträge zu: Aufbau einer Rolle', Brecht praises Laughton's ability 'die widerspruchsvolle Person des großen Physikers in voller Leiblichkeit zu entwickeln' (*16*, p.78). The phrase 'in voller Leiblichkeit' is the crux of the matter, for it is in certain aspects of his appetites and his physicality that one of Galilei's main 'Widersprüche' is to be found. Although it does not seem to have been a characteristic of the real historical figure, Galilei's preoccupation with food and at least some of the pleasures of the flesh is a feature which is repeatedly highlighted by Brecht, both through words and actions. The opening line, 'Stell die Milch auf den Tisch, aber klapp kein Buch zu' (p.7), hardly the most momentous first words in modern drama, acquires its *raison d'être* by signalling this aspect of the man. Galilei wants his pleasures without their disturbing his work. The historical Galilei was generally robust despite the after-effects of early fever, but we have no indication that self-indulgence was a marked feature of the man. So it is worth considering the reasons – there are various ones – why Brecht makes so much of this trait.

The relationship between Galilei's hedonism and his scientific mission has to be seen as an instrumental contradiction, a device to steer audience response. The intelligent spotting of contradictions and pondering their implications was an activity Brecht encouraged in his audiences. His possibly daunting remark about his aim 'die Dialektik zum Genuß zu machen' cites *inter alia* 'der Witz der Widersprüchlichkeit' as one of the main 'Vergnügungen an der Lebendigkeit der Menschen, Dinge und Prozesse'; he adds 'sie steigern die Lebenskunst sowie die Lebensfreudigkeit' (*GW*16, p.702). Given that Brecht's play is specifically entitled *Leben des Galilei*, it is worth bearing in mind this habit of Brecht's of associating aspects of contradictoriness with both liveliness and a fidelity to life: 'lebendig [ist] nur, was widerspruchsvoll ist' (*GW*16, p.928). This is one of the reasons why the ability to highlight contradictions is seen as the strength of a work and those who sought to play down or gloss over contradictions are censured ('Die Darstellungen des bürgerlichen Theaters gehen immer auf die Verschmierung der Widersprüche, auf die Vortäuschung von Harmonie, auf die Idealisierung aus', *GW*16, p.707). But in the final analysis this concern with contradiction is inseparable from ideology. Brecht's thinking about contradiction was deeply indebted to Lenin and Mao Tse-tung. Indeed, in a response to a questionnaire published in *Neue Deutsche Hefte* in 1955 (i.e. when work was well advanced on the third version of his Galilei play), he even voted Mao's *On*

Contradiction the most important work he had read in 1954 (*GW*20, p.343). A copy of the German translation of Lenin's essay on dialectics had been in Brecht's possession since 1925 (in the first volume of the magazine *Unter dem Banner des Marxismus*, edited by Willi Schultz).

According to Mao, 'some contradictions are characterized by open antagonism, others are not' (*52*, p.70), which is a shorthand form of the idea that under capitalism contradictions were antagonistic (i.e. in the short term, destructive), whereas under communism, at least in theory, they would be part of the healthy ongoing dialectic of self-criticism and improvement of the system. The classic statement on this is to be found in Lenin's claim that 'antagonism and contradiction are not [...] one and the same. Under socialism, antagonism will disappear, but contradiction will remain' ('Remarks on N. I. Bukharin's *Economics of the Transitional Period*, quoted in *52*, p.71). Whether the distinction is between 'antagonistic' and 'non-antagonistic' contradictions (Mao) or 'antagonism' and 'contradiction' (Lenin), the implications for our understanding of Brecht are 'largely the same. A work dealing with the problems created by the capitalist system (the subject of most of Brecht's plays) will have as one of its main tasks the highlighting of debilitating contradictions which nevertheless form part of the dialectical process. In Brecht's words: 'Gezeigt werden soll die Veränderbarkeit des Zusammenlebens der Menschen (und damit die Veränderbarkeit des Menschen selbst). Das kann nur geschehen dadurch, daß man das Augenmerk auf alles Unfeste, Flüchtige, Bedingte richtet, kurz auf die Widersprüche in allen Zuständen, welche die Neigung haben, in andere widerspruchsvolle Zustände überzugehen' (*GW*16, p.923).

Given this dialectical context, it is significant that Brecht even made his seemingly innocuous remark linking 'Widersprüchlichkeit' with 'Lebendigkeit' in a sketch entitled 'Dialektische Züge'. The full remark reads 'Da lebendig nur ist, was widerspruchsvoll ist, zeigen die klassischen Werke immer dialektische Züge, hauptsächlich dem Dialektiker'. As this suggests, Brecht tended to use the term 'Widerspruch' (even describing his own kind of drama as 'Widerspruchstheater') as a code word for dialectics. 'Der Dialektiker arbeitet bei allen Erscheinungen und Prozessen das Widerspruchsvolle heraus, er denkt kritisch, das heißt, er bringt in seinem Denken die Erscheinungen in ihre Krise, um sie fassen zu können' (*GW*16, p.794). 'Das Theater entwickelt sich wie alles andere in Widersprüchen. (Das Studium der Dialektik empfiehlt sich [...])' (*GW*16, p.729). The unassuming word 'contradiction' implies both polarity and constructive conflict, the thesis/antithesis starting point for an interpretive model of the struggle between two forces or within a phenomenon, a feature which will move history up one level to a higher stage. If Brechtian theatre has as one of its principal aims the highlighting of such contradictions, then it serves an essentially political end by drawing the audience's attention to the positive aspects of the dialectical conflict. Moreover, since we are not dealing, strictly speaking, with historical plays but with historicizing parables about the twentieth century, the conflict elements being highlighted will have their real analogues in our world rather than simply in Galilei's. In the next chapter, we shall see what this means for Brecht's depiction of the historical process. But the highlighting of contradictory elements also has to be seen as one of the principal strategies in the play's presentation of its central figure.

The contradictions in Galilei's behaviour are clearly not reducible to one single pair of contrasting traits, in the way that Mutter Courage's are: there we see ongoing conflict between motherliness and mercantile drives. Admittedly there are identifiably positive and negative features to Galilei's behaviour, but one of the marked subtleties of *Leben des Galilei* is the extent to which Brecht has for once succeeded in combining positive and negative elements in the same material. ('Das ist eine der großen Schwierigkeiten', Brecht once observed, 'aus dem Helden den Verbrecher herauszuholen', *16*, p.123.) The very things that make Galilei strong also constitute his weakness, whereas the positive and negative aspects of Mutter Courage's behaviour tend to be easily distinguishable and assigned to different parts of the action.

Galilei's materialism is what makes him the observant scientist that he is and in the end destroys him with disastrous consequences for the world around him. Since the actor Charles Laughton, whose work Brecht knew primarily from the film The *Private Life of Henry VIII*, did so much to impose his own physical presence on the figure, it remains tempting to assume that the American version was elaborated in this direction specifically with him in mind. But Brecht had in actual fact been determined from the outset that a robust physicality should be the hallmark of the man. An entry in the *Arbeitsjournal* of 12 August 1938 already expresses dismay at the Germans' ability to conceive of 'einen materialismus ohne sinnlichkeit'; 'der geist verunreinigt sich gleich bei uns, wenn er materie anfaßt' (*1*, p.19). In literature, too, he complains, characters seldom eat, drink or show any other traces of physicality. (Cf. also Section 75 of the *Kleines Organon für das Theater*.) In the letter to Hans Tombrock quoted at the beginning of this chapter, intended to help the artist with the preparations for a series of commissioned drawings of the physicist, we find Brecht anxious to counteract this etherealizing tendency. He stresses that the image of Galilei must break with the popular stereotype of the anaemic, head-in-the-clouds academic: 'Wichtig, daß Du den Galilei nicht idealisierst (Du weißt, Sterngucker, bleicher, vergeistigter Idealistentyp!)' (*16*, p.27). Laughton's Henry VIII and the Hunchback of Notre Dame, Shakespeare's Richard III, even Humpty Dumpty, were the physical models for the new man of science. The fact that Ernst Busch, much wirier than Laughton and strikingly unlike him as an actor, should have been selected to play Galilei in the 1956 East Berlin production is a typically Brechtian move. Not only is Brecht reinterpreting the figure by refusing to have a fat stereotype just to pander to the obvious association between appetite and corporeality (he had repeatedly stressed in his theoretical utterances the dangers of interpreting characters in simplistic terms through their physique, cf. 'Rede des Dramaturgen über Rollenbesetzung', *GW*16, pp.635f.): with Busch's Galilei he was attempting a *Verfremdung* of his previous *Verfremdung* of the stereotypical ascetic intellectual.

Repeated emphasis is placed on the appetites of Galilei: 'ich will die Fleischtöpfe' (p.37); 'Ich schätze die Tröstungen des Fleisches [...]. Ich sage: Genießen ist eine Leistung' (p.88). In production details, too, the point is frequently reinforced: from

Galilei's initial request about the milk right through to the old man's concern in Scene 14 with how the geese should be prepared. Scene 1's lengthy speech about the New Age is delivered with Galilei stripped to the waist, while Andrea rubs his back. He is enjoying the contact of towel on body just as much as he is relishing the eloquence with which he is able to eulogize the New Age. The way he designs his experiments betrays an aesthetic sensibility as well as a pragmatic forte; mind and body are applied to everything he does.

'Galilei ist natürlich kein Falstaff,' Brecht remarked in 'DAS SINNLICHE IN GALILEI';

> als überzeugter Materialist besteht er auf physischen Freuden. Bei der Arbeit würde er zwar nicht trinken; wichtig ist, daß er auf sinnliche Weise *arbeitet*. Es bereitet ihm Genuß, seine Instrumente mit Eleganz zu handhaben. Ein großer Teil seiner Sinnlichkeit ist geistiger Natur. Da gibt es das 'schöne Experiment', [...] dann gibt es in seinen Reden Stellen [...], wo er gute Wörter auswählt und sie abschmeckt wie Gewürze. (*16*, p.28)

On a less elevated plane, Brecht notes Laughton's 'Spiel mit den Händen in den Hosentaschen beim Planen der neuen Forschungen reichte an die Grenze des Anstößigen' (*16*, p.53). That a man who is a materialist must for that reason insist on his physical pleasures sounds a strange assumption. Any connexion between a materialist philosophical position and self-indulgent living seems more like a personal quirk than one of life's 'Gesetzlichkeiten'. But the real problem with this remark is that it concentrates only on the positive side of Galilei's materialism. The Cardinal Inquisitor puts his finger on the obverse aspect, when arguing for showing Galilei the torture instruments: 'Er ist ein Mann des Fleisches. Er würde sofort nachgeben' (p.108). Brecht's play skilfully brings out this contradictory aspect to Galilei's materialism: as his consummate strength and his greatest weakness.

The description of Galilei as 'ein lärmender, vollsaftiger Mann' soon appears too positive to convey the actual contradictory nature of his physicality. The couplet 'Groß ist nicht alles, was ein großer Mann tut / Und Galilei aß gern gut' (p.23) already signals this double-edged factor. So too do many of the references to his appetites as a form of vice. Ludovico's jibe 'Sie werden für immer der Sklave Ihrer Leidenschaften sein' (p.92) is not far wide of the mark. As the Cardinal Inquisitor realizes, his 'Sinnlichkeit' is his Achilles heel. After the recantation, the shower of abuse directed at him ('Weinschlauch! Schneckenfresser!' p.113) is calculated to stress this fact. Galilei's blunt confession 'ich will die Fleischtöpfe' (p.37) was made in order to justify his incautious departure from the Venetian Republic for the material attractions (and dangers) of Florence. As he even admits: 'Ich habe keine Geduld mit den feigen Seelen, die dann von Schwächen sprechen' (p.88); 'ich verachte Leute, deren Gehirn nicht fähig ist, ihren Magen zu füllen' (p.38). He utters the incriminating words 'Ich schätze meine Bequemlichkeit' (p.101) within a few lines of declaring that what people do with his discoveries is no concern of his. Some of these remarks might lead one to suppose that, far from being essentially a virtue, Galilei's gross physicality is another of those devices Dickson sees as being built into the play to make sure the audience do not over-empathize; or that they once more underline the contrast between his laudable intentions and a degrading enslavement to sensuality. If, however, the principal function of this 'Körperlichkeit' were merely either to debunk Galilei or to make him an intriguing amalgam of altruistic and self-gratifying elements, then there would surely be little reason for Brecht's going to such lengths to stress a more eccentric factor in the amalgam: the definite interdependence of physicality and thought; for he has his hero specifically declare at one stage: 'Bei gutem Essen fällt mir am meisten ein' (p.31); and the new pope (a man who knows about such things) says of him: 'Er denkt aus Sinnlichkeit' (108), which goes far beyond simply wanting to get away from the conventional image of the ascetic intellectual.

A clue to the more fundamental significance of this motif can be found in a point Brecht once made in a commentary to Scene 1. A conventional actor, he suggested, would fail to realize the connection between Galilei's 'Wohlbefinden' and his thoughts in the early part of this episode. He would probably want to embroider on the action:

> Selbst ein großer Schauspieler ist nicht in der Lage, das Verfahren des neuen Stückeschreibers zu erkennen. Er wird nach vier Sätzen, bei denen ihm der Rücken gerieben wird, ungeduldig und verlangt andere Tätigkeiten. [...] Er setzt die neuen Gedanken nicht in Beziehung zu dem Wohlbefinden, das der Gelehrte empfindet. Galilei müßte aufhören zu denken, wenn Andrea ihm nicht mehr den Rücken reibt.

Straight away, Brecht goes on to say, in what is the most crucial remark in this context, that 'die Abhängigkeit der Produktion für die Gesellschaft von dem Wohlbefinden des einzelnen, das ihm die Gesellschaft bietet, ist für das Stück von außerordentlicher Wichtigkeit' (*16*, p.31).

On one level, this may seem like an obvious echo of the social contract: if society cannot guarantee Galilei's wellbeing, why should he owe an allegiance to society? On another level, however, there is a more specifically ideological implication to such a symbolic 'Mischung von Körperlichem und Geistigem' (*16*, p.53); for this aspect of Galilei's portrayal reflects the Marxist axiom (first formulated in *Die deutsche Ideologie*) that it is material conditions (the 'Basis') which determine the so-called 'Überbau' of society, and such a concept of the 'Überbau' would include all intellectual activity and awareness of ethical norms. In precisely the same way as the base-superstructure model operates in society, according to Marxist-Leninist theory, so Galilei's behaviour is palpably determined by his 'Wohlbefinden' (or, as often as not, his lack thereof). The mind-body relationship in *Leben des Galilei* becomes an important mirror of the overall 'Überbau'/'Basis' relationship in the world Brecht is depicting. Galilei's life, with its complex intermeshing of matters intellectual with things physical, thus becomes a dramatized illustration of one of Marx's central tenets: 'Es ist nicht das Bewußtsein der Menschen, das ihr Sein, sondern umgekehrt ihr gesellschaftliches Sein, das ihr Bewußtsein bestimmt' (*53*, p.9). The idea was already alluded to in Brecht's 'Anmerkungen zur Oper *Aufstieg und Fall der Stadt Mahagonny*' (1930), which associated the older 'Dramatische Form des Theaters' with the assumption that 'das Denken bestimmt das Sein', whereas in Brecht's Epic Theatre it is said that 'das gesellschaftliche Sein bestimmt das Denken' (*GW*17, p.1010). Change these conditions, such an interpretation implies, and a man like Galilei would not behave as he did.

Galilei's eventual question to Andrea, 'können wir uns der Menge verweigern und doch Wissenschaftler bleiben?' (p.125), raises one of the main unresolved issues of his time and ours: that of the relationship between individual activity and social context. The (rhetorical) question is predicated on an assumption, expressly set out in Galilei's long speech in Scene 14 (but already intimated in the very first scene of *Leben des Galilei*), 'daß das einzige Ziel der Wissenschaft darin besteht, die Mühseligkeit der menschlichen Existenz zu erleichtern' (p.125). There are two aspects to this idea: first, the obvious one that science surrendered to the wrong 'Machthaber' will threaten the lives of 'die Menge' rather than ameliorate them; and second, the wider assumption that all behaviour is essentially political. Galilei castigates himself for not having abided by some non-existent Hippocratic oath which society still needs to invent, but this is a fallacious response. The right kind of society would make such an oath superfluous. Its sole function, if it were to be instituted in the present, would simply be to help bring about the utopia which is the ultimate goal of Brecht's theatre.

Paradoxically *Leben des Galilei* is a play which for its first thirteen scenes goes to great lengths to bring out the extent to which Galilei's negative behaviour is the result of social conditions. Then, in Scene 14, it shows a character bending over backwards in his 'mörderische Analyse' to condemn himself for having betrayed both society and the highest principles of his discipline. Where does this seeming contradiction leave the audience? Certainly we are not meant to absolve Galilei of all responsibility for what has happened. It would be a strange play that allowed him such an extended act of personal condemnation simply in order to discount his words and show that all that he did was the result of social pressures leaving him with no choice in the matter. But as Andrea remarks, his analysis is not 'das letzte Wort' (p.127). If nothing else, Andrea's heroic behaviour in Scene 15 frees the work of any charge of vulgar determinism. People may on the whole be seen to be the victims of socially determining factors (in this sense Galilei is more typical of the norm than Andrea), but they do not have to conform, and Andrea illustrates this point. Instead of crude determinism of the Naturalist kind, we have a situation where a dialectical response is also shown to be possible. For the final scene of the play indicates that people are able to react against conditions rather than simply be manipulated by them. Yet although Andrea's final act of bravery may be merely an individual one at this stage, as he himself says, 'Wir stehen wirklich erst am Beginn' (p.131), a remark which applies to historical progress and not just to the scientific horizons of the time.

Such political issues raised by Galilei's behaviour will be approached once more from a different angle in the next chapter. There we shall again be touching on questions which Brecht explored in slightly different terms in his consideration of the problem of whether or not *Leben des Galilei* should be staged as a tragedy or an optimistic work:

> Es wird sich so für die Theater die Frage erheben, ob sie 'Leben des Galilei' als eine Tragödie oder als ein optimistisches Stück aufführen sollen. Sollen sie sich, was den Grundton betrifft, an die 'Begrüßung der neuen Zeit' durch Galilei in der ersten Szene oder an gewisse Partien der vierzehnten Szene halten? Nach den herrschenden Regeln des Stückebaus muß der Schluß eines Stückes schwerer gewogen werden. Aber das Stück ist nicht nach diesen Regeln gebaut. Das Stück zeigt den Anbruch einer neuen Zeit und versucht, einige Vorurteile über den Anbruch einer neuen Zeit zu revidieren. (*16*, p.13)

Transferring this argument to the play's presentation of Galilei's behaviour, one could conclude that there is a danger of placing too much emphasis on Galilei's eventual self-condemnation, both on the grounds that it does not square with the full picture we have been shown in previous scenes and because it lacks historico-political wisdom. (Its metaphorical reference to a Hippocratic oath is tantamount to evidence of an inevitably inadequate political interpretation on the protagonist's part.) Galilei may be partly correct to blame himself for the way he behaved, though what is at stake is not just the recantation in Scene 13, but also the various other peccadillos and acts of betrayal over the years. Only the audience will be able to assess his mistakes in context, though still without relieving Galilei of his share of responsibility. Expecting one man to bear the sole blame for holding up the progress of science or assuming that a single elaborate and self-indulgent act of self-criticism in Scene 14 sets things aright would be an inadequate response. As Brecht remarked, 'seine Selbstanalyse darf unter keinen Umständen [...] dazu mißbraucht werden, mit Hilfe von Selbstvorwürfen den Helden dem Publikum sympathisch zu machen' (*16*, p.36). Humpty Dumpty cannot be put together again, that is sure. But, of course, Galilei's reinstatement is not the play's concern at this stage; it is in reasserting the promise of 'der Anbruch der neuen Zeit' and, whatever the opposition (be it Nazi or US capitalist), in suggesting ways of putting a fractured society together again and finding the road back to a secularized, socialist version of the Paradise implied by the Fall metaphor. For it is above all society's 'Sündenfall', not just one individual's, 'große Maschine' though he may be, that Brecht's play has been exploring through the medium of 'der Fall Galilei'.

3. *Astronomy, History and Politics*

Leben des Galilei is enmeshed in the complexities of actual historical events to a greater degree than any of Brecht's previous plays, and communicates a clearer sense of the Marxist view of history as a dialectical process than is to be found anywhere else in his work. Although Brecht engaged in an extensive preparatory study of the contemporary Italian background, of Galilei's life and his significance for the history of science, strict fidelity to fact was by no means an absolute guiding principle. He was quite prepared to modify his material for aesthetic or ideological reasons, mainly because *Leben des Galilei* was about a twentieth-century predicament, regardless of how successful it might be in bringing Galileo's own age to life. The result, far from being a 'period play' in any traditional sense, does not set out to evoke another epoch with a full panoply of scholarly, authenticated detail or to exploit pageant for the kind of escape-into-the-past that had been fashionable in exile circles in the 1930s. The work's artistic treatment of its historical subject matter is on the whole innovative, although in substance it betrays a profound indebtedness to orthodox Marxism-Leninism.

One way of accounting for the playwright's turning to a seventeenth-century theme at a time when Europe was on the brink of a cataclysm is as a distancing strategy. A less familiar past can function as a framework within which to explore contemporary problems. Interpreted thus *Leben des Galilei* reveals itself to be a more subtle example of Brecht's by then well-tried technique of transposition (the 'geographische Verfremdung' of *Der gute Mensch von Sezuan* and *Arturo Ui* or the 'historische Verfremdung' of *Mutter Courage und ihre Kinder* as well as *Der kaukasische Kreidekreis*). Fashioning a parable from the materials of distant – and distancing – history, rather than inventing a parabolic setting, creates a more tangible set of socio-political issues than one encounters in such imprecise geographical transpositions as Brecht's own *Die Rundköpfe und die Spitzköpfe* or many of the *Modellstücke* of Frisch and Dürrenmatt, where the abstractness of the method often leaves one paddling in platitudinous shallows.

To understand what Brecht set out to achieve with his Galilei play, we should, however, approach it not just as a parable, but in relation to the playwright's concept of *Historisierung*. 'Bei der *Historisierung* wird ein bestimmtes Gesellschaftssystem vom Standpunkt eines anderen Gesellschaftssystems aus betrachtet. Die Entwicklung der Gesellschaft ergibt die Gesichtspunkte' (*GW*16, p.653). By virtue of the fact that history is conceived of as always on the move, with society continually changing, *Historisierung* creates a constructive awareness of the world's 'Veränderbarkeit': 'Was ist, war nicht immer und wird nicht immer sein' (*GW*16, p.656). Demonstrating the relativity of another age's problems (be they astronomical, social or political) induces in the audience a general awareness of 'das Historische eines bestimmten gesellschaftlichen Zustandes' (*GW*16, p.631), thereby counteracting the assumption that the majority of problems are 'zeitlos' and therefore insoluble. *Historisierung* is an aesthetic technique for encouraging a less fatalistic attitude. We are invited to see not only past, but also present events as 'historische Vorgänge' (in Brecht's sense):

> Historische Vorgänge sind einmalige, vorübergehende, mit bestimmten Epochen verbundene Vorgänge. Das Verhalten der Personen in ihnen ist nicht ein schlechthin menschliches, unwandelbares, es hat bestimmte Besonderheiten, *es hat durch den Gang der Geschichte Überholtes und Überholbares und ist der Kritik vom Standpunkt der jeweilig darauffolgenden Epoche unterworfen*. Die ständige Entwicklung entfremdet uns das Verhalten der vor uns Geborenen. (*GW*15, p.347, my emphasis)

'Das Feld muß in seiner historischen Relativität gekennzeichnet werden können', according to the *Kleines Organon für das Theater*

(*GW*16, p.678). The challenge for the author of *Leben des Galilei* lay in establishing, within the confines of fifteen short scenes, the 'Zeitgebundenheit' of his material and that of its modern analogues. By no means all of his plays reach the sophisticated level of *Historisierung* to be found here. *Mutter Courage und ihre Kinder* also returns to the seventeenth century to illustrate the mercantile nature of war. But instead of bringing out the historical relativity of its subject matter, the central juxtaposition simply creates the impression that the problems of the Thirty Years' War – aggression, corruption, mercenary-mindedness, economic exploitation masquerading as fighting in a good cause – are in fact still with us today. The end result, despite the use of the past as a test tube within which to observe the problems of the present, is that we are left with parallels and a sense of historical stasis.

Historisierung is the operative factor behind the use of the seventeenth century in *Leben des Galilei*, not just for cognitive reasons but in order to prepare modern audiences for 'eingreifendes Denken' (*GW*18, p.236). As Brecht once put it (alluding to Marx's eleventh *Feuerbachthese*): 'Ich wollte auf das Theater den Satz anwenden, daß es nicht nur darauf ankommt, die Welt zu interpretieren, sondern sie zu verändern' (*GW*16, p.815).

Very early on we are presented with a sense of history, in the words of the orthodox Marxist-Leninist conception, as a 'gesetzmäßiger Entwicklungsprozeß der Gesellschaft vom Niederen zum Höheren' (*47*, p.402). This is the function of the speech in Scene 1 where Galilei greets the new world with infectious enthusiasm: 'jetzt fahren wir heraus, Andrea, in großer Fahrt. Denn die alte Zeit ist herum, und es ist eine neue Zeit' (p.8). The euphoric words that follow are erected upon a series of contrasts: between 'sitzen' and 'fahren', 'Glaube' and 'Zweifel', restriction and open spaces, stasis and flux. Just as bold new Columbuses are setting out in search of fresh continents and astronomers are rethinking the dynamics of the solar system, so history is all movement and adventure. People are no longer content to remain cocooned in a comforting recurrence of the old, tried and over familiar. A commitment to knowledge is already associated with bravery.

Finding himself 'an der Schwelle einer neuen Zeit' (*16*, p.7), Galilei rejoices as a member of the human race, not just in his capacity as physicist or astronomer. He is not primarily interested in discoveries for their own sake, but in how they will help to create a better world, above all for the downtrodden: 'als junger Mensch, sah ich, wie ein paar Bauleute eine tausendjährige Gepflogenheit, Granitblöcke zu bewegen, durch eine neue und zweckmäßigere Anordnung der Seile ersetzten, nach einem Disput von fünf Minuten. Da und dann wußte ich: die alte Zeit ist herum, und es ist eine neue Zeit' (p.9). What follows, with its visionary imagery and Old Testament confidence of tone, has the ring of secularized prophecy: 'Ich sage voraus, daß noch zu unsern Lebzeiten auf den Märkten von Astronomie gesprochen werden wird. Selbst die Söhne der Fischweiber werden in die Schulen laufen' (p.10). (Note the dynamism of the imagery, having them eagerly *running* to school, not just *sitting* in classrooms.) There are moments where we glimpse an egalitarian future where Church and aristocracy have been toppled. 'Der Papst, die Kardinäle, die Fürsten, die Gelehrten, Kapitäne, Kaufleute, Fischweiber und Schulkinder glaubten, unbeweglich in dieser kristallenen Kugel zu sitzen. Aber jetzt [...]', (p.8). The remark starts by paying lip service to the social hierarchy of the day, beginning with the Pope and descending through the various strata (gradually deprived of their definite articles), but this is simply in order to emphasize that they are *all*, from schoolchild to Holy Father, mistaken. All have been demoted from their place at the centre of the universe. The heliocentric system is already presented in a manner suggesting democratizing possibilities. The contagious idea 'alles bewegt sich' (p.9) is destined to leave no part of the social order untouched. Various disrespectful images (looking beneath the robes of the mighty, papal fallibility) indicate that what is being contemplated is a more far-reaching change than anything confined to astronomy or physics.

However, Brecht would not have been the ingenious dramatist he was, if there were not more to Galilei's speech than this. As various commentators have argued (*25*, *31*, *33*), Galilei's euphoria is signally premature. His naive historical confidence is the result of a tendency to overestimate the persuasiveness of reason and misguage his opponents' intransigence. The next twelve scenes offer limited justification for the dominant mood of Scene 1. Nevertheless, this does not totally invalidate Galilei's optimism, for although the opposition may triumph in the short term, ultimately, according to Brecht's Marxist view, the dialectical laws according to which history operates ensure that the outcome of the conflict will eventually be positive. This is why we are also meant to see in Scene 1's hymn to the New Age a variation on Brecht's optimism about his own Golden Age, 'golden' because the age was, following the Communist Manifesto's view of Marxism as a 'scientific' ideology, the greatest 'wissenschaftliches Zeitalter' to date. 'Die neue Wissenschaft, die sich mit dem Wesen der menschlichen Gesellschaft befaßt und die vor etwa hundert Jahren begründet wurde', as the *Neues Organon* puts it (*GW*16, p.670): this was Brecht's equivalent of Galilei's new astronomical awareness.

Yet in a draft foreword Brecht refers to the 'schnell wachsende Finsternis' of a period 'umgeben von blutigen Taten und nicht weniger blutigen Gedanken, der zunehmenden Barbarei, die unhemmbar in den vielleicht größten und furchtbarsten Krieg aller Zeiten zu führen scheint'. Under such circumstances, he finds it 'schwer, eine Haltung einzunehmen, die sich für Leute an der Schwelle einer neuen und glücklichen Zeit schicken mag' (*16*, p.9). But, for all his hesitation ('Deutet nicht alles darauf hin, daß es Nacht wird, und nichts, daß eine neue Zeit beginnt?'), even the first version of *Leben des Galilei* ends with the rousing words 'Wir stehen wirklich erst am Beginn' (*BFA*5, p.109).

Brecht's Galilei story hinges on a scientific debate comprehensible to the lay person: does the sun rotate around the earth or vice versa? As well as astronomical controversy, signs of social change can also be detected in Galilei's first long speech, hence the importance of the new pulley system for the Siena dock workers. Papal authority is questioned in scientific matters, the crucial repercussion being that his supreme position in the feudal hierarchy comes under fire. Here we already see Brecht rising to one of his greatest challenges: to make something as seemingly apolitical as astronomy (the Cardinal Inquisitor calls it an 'abliegende Wissenschaft', p.106) into a socially relevant, even revolutionary issue. After Hiroshima, this could partly be done by stressing the common discipline. Physicists fathered the atomic bomb, therefore Galileo must be presented as a physicist, rather than as an astronomer *tout court*. (*Leben des Physikers Galilei* was at one stage the play's projected title.) Nevertheless, the historical links the author needed to establish, first between his hero and the head-below-the-parapet intellectuals of the Third Reich and later with those responsible for the development and use of nuclear weapons, had to be worked on. They are not as self-evident as the analogy between Inquisition and Gestapo. It is a task Brecht tackled in three main ways: (i) by making much (especially in the carnival scene) of the parallel between celestial harmony and repressively ordered earthly hierarchies; (ii) by showing that the legitimization of knowledge is part of the power structure and therefore that it is not so much astronomy per se that is intrinsically political but the Church's monopoly at the time on all knowledge; and (iii) by making his Galilei sympathetic to the plight of the lower classes and an egalitarian at heart, traits which the real figure possessed to a restricted degree.

'Vielleicht werde ich sie die "Mediceischen Gestirne" taufen, nach dem Großherzog von Florenz', Galilei remarks, upon discovering the four moons of Jupiter (pp.36f). His decision to name these 'ERSCHEINUNGEN (AM HIMMEL), WELCHE DAS KOPERN-IKANISCHE SYSTEM BEWEISEN' (p.27) after the house of his prospective patron may at first look like an astute piece of sycophancy, effectively smoothing the way for his move to Florence. But there is more to his ploy than this. To append to the 'Trabanten' the innocuous label 'Gestirne' and baptize them after the powerful Medicis is a political insurance policy. However, the plan quickly runs into trouble, as we see from a remark made by the Philosopher in the next scene: 'wir sind vollkommen überzeugt, Herr Galilei, daß weder Sie noch sonst jemand es wagen würde, Sterne mit dem erlauchten Namen des Herrscherhauses zu schmücken, deren Existenz nicht über allen Zweifel erhaben wäre' (p.47). What was intended to protect the new discovery from Galilei's opponents evidently backfires. Increasingly through the rest of the play, astronomy becomes political because Rome ('geistliche Obrigkeit, letzte wissenschaftliche Instanz [...] weltliche Obrigkeit, letzte politische Instanz', *16*, p.14) seeks to retain control over every area of knowledge, especially the potentially heretical or socially destabilizing.

One of the main political flashpoints between the ecclesiastical Establishment and the upholders of the new heliocentric system lay in astronomy's challenge to the Bible. Matters really came to a head in a disputation at Florence in the presence of one of Galilei's pupils, Benedetto Castelli, centring on Joshua 10. 13, where the sun is said to have 'stood still' in Gibeon. The amalgam of biblical and classical sources brought to bear against the real historical Galilei constituted one of the main pieces of 'evidence' why the Ptolemaic theory must be right and the Copernicans wrong. But, as Brecht's Galilei remarks, 'man zitiert Aristoteles, (aber) der Mann hatte kein Fernrohr!' (p.48). Now that the instrument has produced discoveries in support of the heliocentric theory, the debate has become essentially one between scientific evidence and the Word of the Bible. But wisely Brecht's Galilei confines himself to the status of Aristotle's teachings rather than that of Holy Scripture: 'der Glaube an die Autorität des Aristoteles ist eine Sache, Fakten, die mit Händen zu greifen sind, eine andere' (p.48).

In making use of this historical debate in Scene 6, Brecht chooses to personalize it in a new way. For a start, the objection is voiced in Galilei's presence instead of being mediated via a pupil, though the pro-Bible position is devalued by being put into the mouth of an unattractive, thin monk: 'EIN SEHR DÜNNER MÖNCH *kommt mit einer aufgeschlagenen Bibel nach vorn, fanatisch den Finger auf eine Stelle stoßend*: Was steht hier in der Schrift? "Sonne, stehe still zu Gibeon [...]!" Wie kann die Sonne stillstehen, wenn sie sich überhaupt nicht dreht, wie diese Ketzer behaupten? Lügt die Schrift?' (p.60). Galilei keeps his counsel at this juncture. As the monk's words indicate, the issue has potentially become one of heresy, not merely that of supporting the unacceptable one of two rival astronomical theories. The shadow of the dead Giordano Bruno

looms across the scene. At best Galilei can only bide his time, hoping
for a more sympathetic hearing from his intellectual peers, which, of
course, Clavius's favourable verdict provides at the end of the scene.
But general acceptance does not follow in the wake of Clavius's
endorsement. Growing popular sympathy for Galilei's ideas and the
Church's disquiet about their implications led in 1616 to the placing
of Copernicus' *De revolutionibus orbium coelestium* on the Index:
'Das Heilige Offizium hat [...] beschlossen, daß die Lehre des
Kopernikus, nach der die Sonne Zentrum der Welt [!] und beweglich
ist, töricht, absurd und ketzerisch im Glauben ist' (p.69). This may
seem a curious ploy, given that by this time Galilei is really the one
in need of muzzling. But the move is intended as a warning shot
across Galilei's bow. In reality, the ban on Copernicus was lifted four
years later, and with the coming to the throne of Pope Urban VIII, a
more favourable climate set in. Brecht's Scene 9 partly echoes this by
having the hero 'ERMUTIGT, SEINE FORSCHUNGEN AUF DEM
VERBOTENEN FELD WIEDER AUFZUNEHMEN', encouraged, that is,
by the installation of the new pope (p.80). But in Brecht's version this
was little more than a false lull in the storm. The new astronomy
remained under attack as a threat to the temporal and theological
status quo, and a power struggle developed between the Church and
those pleading for the autonomy of knowledge in the dawning new
age of unfettered scientific discovery. Obviously, it is at the point
where Galilei is forced to recant that the conflict emerges in all its
ruthlessness. Before that, Brecht charts the relatively civilized way in
which control could be asserted by indirect means – what he in his
'Bemerkungen zu einzelnen Szenen' (*16*, p.32) refers to as 'die Kunst
der Fingerzeige' (in other words, a nod from the Vatican is as good as
a thumbs-down from the Inquisition). Even the bantering battle of
quotations between Galilei and the Cardinals in Scene 9 amounts to
little more than a flexing of muscles within the civilized atmosphere
of high society. Etiquette for the time being cosmeticizes the face of
State censorship.

     To appreciate the full force of this depiction of the Church's
control over the dissemination of truth, however, one has to see it in
the context of the specifically Marxist conception of power. To quote

Carver, Marx 'emphasizes that the ruling class does not rule by brute force alone. If it did, it would not rule for long. The longevity and stability of the ruling class's dominance are due to a second and arguably more important factor: its ability to influence, if not control, the thoughts, the beliefs and ideas – the "consciousness" of the working class' (*44*, p.130). Not only does *Leben des Galilei* show ideology working to the benefit of the ruling class, we also see how 'Höflichkeit' and political innuendo allow them to apply coercion and yet mask their aggression behind genteel codes of acceptable conduct. It may be more than a decade since the 'Moritat von Mackie Messer' had presented the image of a gentleman gangster, wearing white gloves to conceal the blood on his hands, who was really a shark with concealed teeth, but the image of disguised power remains largely unchanged. When practising their 'Kunst der Fingerzeige' in Scene 7, Bellarmin and Barberini wear the masks of lamb and dove. ('One can't live in Italy without wearing a mask', Paolo Sarpi, a Venetian contemporary of Galilei's, once observed, *54*, p.9). The cardinals take off their masks to offer him an ominous warning, but the mask image of state-sanctioned power is reasserted at the end of the scene.

The extent to which power is a matter of ideology, or as Engels would have it, the oppressed have internalized the 'falsches Bewußtsein' of the dominant ideology, comes out most clearly in the scene with the Little Monk (whose title Grimm (*14*, p.155) sees as a *Verfremdung* of the phrase 'der kleine Mann'). Here is someone fielding all the stock arguments for maintaining a *status quo*, both against his own self-interest and that of the Campagna peasants whom he wants to shield. The Little Monk, who had delivered Clavius's verdict in the previous scene and is now puzzled by the contradiction between the Church's gag on Galilei and the fact that his discoveries have been upheld, is introduced as 'eines armen Bauern Kind' (p.74), yet the discussion takes place in, of all locations, a palace. The arguments the Monk presents in favour of retaining a 'gewisse Ordnung', even in the travails of the Campagna labourers, are refuted by Galilei, who cuts through both psychological and theological rationalizations of the situation in order to expose the underlying exploitation: 'Ihre Campagnabauern bezahlen die Kriege, die der Stellvertreter des milden Jesus in Spanien und Deutschland führt. Warum stellt er die Erde in den Mittelpunkt des Universums? Damit der Stuhl Petri im Mittelpunkt der Erde stehen kann!' (pp.76f.). As in *Mutter Courage und ihre Kinder*, religion serves as a smokescreen for power politics and profit. Arguably, Galilei emerges as more of a political commentator in this scene than virtually anywhere else in the play; and he does so by invoking arguments about religion as the opium of the masses and as the legitimation of the ruling class in a way which makes his thinking sound like Marxism *avant la lettre*. Again, the play brings together the issues of the seventeenth century and the perspectives of the twentieth century, of astronomy and modern politics.

If there is one place where *Leben des Galilei* makes the relationship between its historical material and our own period disturbingly clear, it is at that moment in Scene 14 where Galilei turns from postmortem to prophecy. Addressing his former pupil and colleague in the collective familiar 'Ihr'-form, presumably as a fellow member of the scientific fraternity, he sententiously predicts a time when scientists will be able to bring about mass destruction. These words are a reminder of the extent to which Galilei's betrayal of his ethical responsibility prefigures the way in which those who should have known better have surrendered to various modern *Machtpolitiker*. But this is not the only moment where prophetic elements leapfrog the intervening years to establish connexions between a fictitious seventeenth century and our later world.

In Scene 3, in response to Galilei's 'Heute ist der 10. Januar 1610. Die Menschheit trägt in ihr Journal ein: Himmel abgeschafft' (p.28), Sagredo inquires 'wo ist Gott in deinem Weltsystem?'. Galilei comes out with an answer which again seems to point well beyond 1610: 'In uns oder nirgends' (p.33). This may sound strange, coming from a man who elsewhere claims to be 'ein gläubiger Sohn der Kirche' (p.68). But then, even more so is the iconoclastic remark 'Himmel abgeschafft'. Brecht may be right to say '[es] entspricht der historischen Wahrheit, wenn der *Galilei* des Stückes sich niemals direkt gegen die Kirche wendet' (*BFA*24, p.238), since his play does not over-polarize the situation by making Galilei an agnostic or an atheist, although a comparison between what he feels free to say to Sagredo and what he is obliged to say to the powerful Cardinal Bellarmin suggests that he does not always speak with one voice on theological matters. When he senses it is safe to do so, Galilei comes very close to agnosticism. 'In uns oder nirgends' in fact reflects two stages of later history: the Protestant emphasis on 'in uns' that is so soon to give rise to religious wars across Europe and in some places topple the edifice of Catholic power; the 'oder nirgends' points forward to the later doctrinaire atheist position of Marxism-Leninism.

Such historical anticipations are not confined to Galilei, where they might simply suggest a lone figure ahead of his time. When, in Scene 4, young Andrea and the boy-prince Cosmo de Medici '*beginnen zu raufen und kugeln sich* [...] *auf dem Boden*' (p.43), breaking the Ptolemaic model in the process, the fisticuffs between a son of the people and an aristocrat become a harbinger of the great revolutions to come in France and Russia. The fact that Brecht has modified the Grand Duke's name from 'Cosimo' to 'Cosmo' points to his symbolic significance: while he is at present a microcosm of the powers that rule the world, his world is soon to come to an end.

In Scene 6, Darwinism is likewise anticipated. The alarmed Thin Monk predicts: 'Wir werden den Tag erleben, wo sie sagen: Es gibt auch nicht Mensch und Tier, der Mensch selber ist ein Tier, es gibt nur Tiere!' (p.61). At the end of his encounter with the Little Monk, Galilei says: 'ich ließe mich zehn Klafter unter der Erde in einen Kerker einsperren, zu dem kein Licht mehr dringt, wenn ich dafür erführe, was das ist: Licht' (p.79). Here, the audience is doubtless meant to recall later physicists, including Newton and Goethe, who will offer answers that Galilei could only dream of giving.

A few anachronisms point back to previous history, rather than presenting Galilei's age in the context of what is still to come. Scene 14 contains reminiscences of the retreating Luther's manoeuvrings at the end of the Peasants' Revolt. When Virginia reads back some of his words ('Anlangend die Stellungnahme der Heiligen Kirche zu den Unruhen im Arsenal von Venedig stimme ich überein mit der

Haltung Kardinal Spolettis gegenüber den aufrührerischen Seilern',
pp.116f.), the mock enthusiasm with which Galilei expresses his
approval recalls Luther's capitulation in the previous century and
reminds us that the revolts of the future will not result in such abject
surrender on the part of those who should be giving the
revolutionaries moral support.

The song preceding the Shrove Tuesday carnival procession
contains a caricature of the present hierarchical world ('Um die
Vorderen die Hinteren / Wie im Himmel, so auf Erden' etc., pp.94f.),
but also points forward to an age when such conditions will no longer
prevail:

> Wer wär nicht auch mal gern sein eigner Herr und Meister?
> Der Pächter tritt jetzt in den Hintern
> Den Pachtherrn ohne Scham
> Die Pächtersfrau gibt ihren Kindern
> Milch, die der Pfaff bekam. (p.96)

The ballad-singer's rabble-rousing *Moritat* is explicitly introduced as
'ein Vorgeschmack der Zukunft' (p.94). But while one can appreciate
that this is the scene which most explicitly foretells the future
theological and social implications of Galilei's discoveries, it is only
a more explicit version of the many other moments in *Leben des
Galilei* where we are afforded a 'taste of the future'.

One of them, Scene 15, is dominated by a contrast between
Andrea's rationality and the superstition of the children playing at the
border check-point. Die alte Marina, whose cottage is nearby, is
assumed by most of the children to be a witch. One of their number, a
veritable Doubting Thomas in the Galilei-Brecht mould, rejects these
tales of her taking to her broomstick at night: 'Wie soll sie denn
durch die Luft fliegen?' (p.129). The boy's question is left
unanswered for a long time, but Andrea eventually returns to it right
at the end of the scene, when he has crossed over the border and can
at last afford to draw this much attention to himself:

ANDREA *sich umwendend* [...] ich habe dir noch nicht
auf deine Frage geantwortet, Giuseppe. Auf einem Stock
kann man nicht durch die Luft fliegen. Er müßte
zumindest eine Maschine dran haben. Aber eine solche
Maschine gibt es noch nicht. Vielleicht wird es sie nie
geben, da der Mensch zu schwer ist. Aber natürlich, man
kann es nicht wissen. Wir wissen bei weitem nicht genug,
Giuseppe. (p.131)

The nudging knowingness of Andrea's 'noch nicht' and his
ruminations about being on the threshold of fresh discoveries may
not be Brecht at his most subtle, but the remark is more complex than
it appears to be on the surface. The contrast here is not simply
between superstition and 'Vernunft'. The image of the aeroplane in
the final speech of the play takes up the idea that Man's 'Jubelschrei
über irgendeine neue Errungenschaft' may one day be answered by a
universal 'Entsetzensschrei'. Planes will not simply symbolize the
triumph of technological inventiveness over gravity (a counter-image
to Galilei's own 'Fall'); the reference also emphasizes that it was this
particular 'neue Errungenschaft' that dropped bombs on Guernica
(Picasso's painting of that name was one of the illustrations in the
theatre programme to the Berliner Ensemble's production of the play)
and rained devastation on so many populations during the Second
World War, as well as the fact that it was from the air that the atomic
bomb was released on two Japanese cities. Andrea's words, which
may at first seem like no more than a rather precocious prophecy of
the future, in fact bear echoes of the betrayals of the recent past as
well.

However, not all the play's prolepses are this transparent.
When Ludovico abandons Virginia, he is subjected to an angry
outburst from Andrea and Federzoni:

LUDOVICO Guten Tag. *Er geht.*
ANDREA Und empfehlen Sie uns allen Marsilis!
FEDERZONI Die der Erde befehlen stillzustehen, damit

ihre Schlösser nicht herunterpurzeln!
ANDREA Und den Cenzis und den Villanis!
FEDERZONI Den Cervillis!
ANDREA Den Lecchis!
FEDERZONI Den Pirleonis!
ANDREA Die dem Papst nur die Füße küssen wollen,
     wenn er damit das Volk niedertritt! (p.92)

Resentment has clearly been building up; they have made a mental note of the names of their oppressors (virtually a revolutionary hit list), and the image is of a nobility sensing that its castles will tumble, if the heavenly order is disturbed. Another 'Vorgeschmack der Zukunft' is offered by Galilei's remarks on chess. 'Wie könnt Ihr noch immer das alte Schach spielen?', he asks two of Bellarmin's secretaries in Scene 7. 'Eng, eng. Jetzt spielt man doch so, daß die größeren Figuren über alle Felder gehen. Der Turm so – *er zeigt es* – und der Läufer so – und die Dame so und so. Da hat man Raum und kann Pläne machen' (p.65). Since chess is a hierarchical game patterned on the feudal social order (king, queen, knights etc.), Galilei's pooh-poohing of its constricting rules is a further anticipation of the future. The secretary's reply reinforces the feeling in so much of the rest of the play that the time is not yet ripe for such boldness: 'Das entspricht nicht unsern kleinen Gehältern, wissen Sie. Wir können nur solche Sprünge machen. *Er zieht einen kleinen Zug*' (p.65). Nevertheless, this poor pen-pusher knew exactly what Galilei was really talking about, and it was not chess.

Brecht was suspicious of surfaces because they tended to be deceptive. His classic declaration that 'eine Photographie der Kruppwerke oder der AEG ergibt beinahe nichts über diese Institute' (*GW*18, p.161) is an argument against surface realism's inability to penetrate to 'die Vorgänge hinter den Vorgängen, die das Schicksal bestimmen' (*GW*15, p.257). A comparable way of getting below the surface is one of the main features of Brecht's treatment of history in *Leben des Galilei*. As he remarks in the context of his *Coriolanus* adaptation, the goal is not faithfully to reproduce history but to X-ray it, 'ein Stück durchleuchteter Geschichte zu behandeln' (*GW*16, p.888). The process of X-raying allows the bone structure of the historical process and thus the shape of the future to emerge from what appears to be a play about no more than a relatively contained period. To this effect, many of Galilei's remarks turn out to be quotations from thinkers who made them well after the time of their being quoted. When Galilei says 'Ich halte dafür, daß das einzige Ziel der Wissenschaft darin besteht, die Mühseligkeit der menschlichen Existenz zu erleichtern' (p.125), earlier sentiments from Bacon's *Novum Organum* have been put into his mouth; but when he suggests that if God did not exist, He would have to be invented, then it is Voltaire who is being echoed. Similarly, Galilei's belief in the 'sanfte Gewalt der Vernunft' often makes him sound like an Enlightenment rationalist rather than a representative of the seventeenth century. Moreover, as Livingstone has convincingly argued (*26*, p.254), given the association of Marxism with reason in Brecht's thinking ('Er ist vernünftig, jeder versteht ihn', *GW*2, p.852), we may be able to glimpse here a foreshadowing not only of the Enlightenment but also of Marxism-Leninism. The effect of such historically omniscient montage is to assign 'der Fall Galilei' its place within a historical chain leading from his own time to the present.

Apart from X-raying it to bring out the teleology, Brecht also often simplifies his historical material. Simplification was always one of his preferred methods to clarify the thrust of the subject matter: 'Damit das Verhalten der Figuren des Dramas so deutlich gezeigt werden kann, daß der Zuschauer die politische Bedeutung dieses Verhaltens voll erfassen kann, sind einige Vereinfachungen nötig' (*BFA*24, p.172). The author draws attention to some repercussions of this selective approach in his discussion of the Church's presentation in the play. 'Das Stück verzichtet [...] darauf, die von der neueren Geschichtswissenschaft [...] festgestellten Fälschungen in dem Protokoll von 1616 durch die Inquisitionsbehörde von 1633 zu berücksichtigen.' (That this is a large can of worms has since been shown by Redondi in *55*.) 'Der Urteilsspruch von 1633 wurde zweifellos durch sie juristisch ermöglicht. Wer den eben skizzierten Standpunkt versteht, wird begreifen, daß es dem Verfasser auf diese juristische Seite des Prozesses nicht ankam' (*BFA*24, p.239). Brecht also notes that, historically, bad blood existed between the real Pope

Urban VIII and Galilei, not least because in his *Dialogue of the Two Great World Systems* of 1632 the real Galilei had put some of the Pope's arguments into the mouth of a character unflatteringly called Simplicio. But such personal animosity would be out of place in a play about history as class conflict; hence, as Brecht puts it, 'das Stück geht daran vorüber' (*BFA*24, p.239). Such streamlining is tantamount to cooking the historical books for ideological effect. Brecht's version of the events of Galilei's life is a Marxist interpretation, and, as even fellow Marxist Schumacher points out, he sometimes got things wrong, but more often deliberately gave them a new political slant. Just like the writers of Soviet and GDR Socialist Realism, he can claim in his defence that he is merely allowing future developments to shine through the surface of his depiction. So, if history is being re-emphasized to create a *geschichtsphilosophisches Modell* rather than being geared to a faithful presentation of the facts, then we need to recognize the processes by which this is brought about in the play.

Four main patterns can be detected in Brecht's appropriation of history: *streamlining* (the elimination of cluttering detail); *ideologically motivated selection* (usually in the form of the suppression of political facts); *polarization* (making sharper than it was in historical reality the essential implications of the clash between Galilei and the Church); and *invention* (adding episodes, characters and details which are not historically vouchsafed).

Brecht himself pointed to some examples of *streamlining* when indicating his reasons for not addressing the legal complexities of Galilei's hearing before the Inquisition and the bad blood between Pope and scientist. The story, probably apocryphal, that Galilei muttered the words 'Eppur si muove' ('But it still moves') after recanting is also not included in the final version, although Brecht had used the title *Die Erde bewegt sich doch* in an early draft. It would scarcely have suited Brecht's conception of a man recanting out of naked fear to have him muttering such a remark beneath his breath. This would have made him more the kind of figure Andrea wanted him to be and subsequent legend made of him. (The closest we get to this idea is with Galilei's 'Alles bewegt sich' in Scene 1, but that sums up the general *Zeitgeist* and is merely said to Andrea.)

On the whole, streamlining tends to remove complicating material without seriously distorting events. To have done justice to the fact that the real Galilei, who was born in Pisa (i.e. in Tuscany), had already spent some of his early years in Florence, and, even when a Professor at the University of Padua, used to return to Florence each summer to give lessons to Cosimo de' Medici, would only have blurred the play's clear-cut picture of a man who gives up the freedoms of the Venetian Republic for the fleshpots of Florence. Also, the fawning letter he writes from Padua to the Grand Duke Cos(i)mo would read differently if it were known to have been written to someone he knew and with whom he already had a close working relationship. For similar reasons, no use can be made of the fact that the real Galilei had already made the acquaintance of Cardinal Barberini in Rome as early as 1611. The phases of Galilei's passage towards the Inquisition's grasp have to be kept more clearly distinct than this. Also the fact that the real Cardinal Bellarmini died at about the same time as the old Pope is ignored by Brecht. Instead of sweeping away the old guard all at once, *Leben des Galilei* allows for much more overlap between the old and the incipient new order, and as a consequence puts both Galilei and the Pope himself in significantly greater jeopardy.

As in Brecht's play, Galilei's final and most important work, the *Discorsi* (*Discourses on Two New Sciences*), was written at Arcetri and smuggled out to Holland (an attractive detail, given the importance of the Amsterdam publishing houses as centres of exile publication during the 1930s). But whereas Brecht has the manuscript smuggled out by Andrea, it was in reality secreted away by an ambassador uncle of the Grand Duke of Tuscany. In Brecht's version of events, Cosmo comes through as a fair-weather friend who disowns Galilei when his notoriety becomes too uncomfortable. But his real historical counterpart was less fickle; and the following Grand Duke, Ferdinand the son of Cosimo, was in his turn a pillar of support for Galilei during his confinement at Arcetri, so it is logical to find a member of his family being instrumental in rescuing the

Discorsi in real life. Although Brecht presents a differentiated view of the opposition to Galilei (among representatives of the Church in the play we come across favourably inclined figures like Clavius, the Papal Astronomer, and the Little Monk), there are limits to his even-handedness. It may be wishful thinking to have the *Discorsi* saved by a working-class character rather than a member of the aristocracy, but this is the final scene of the play and it would hardly have suited the author to make such a grateful acknowledgement for the help of the ruling class at this late stage. In any case, Galilei, who came from a well-educated patrician family with many aristocratic connexions, has had his social roots blurred for most of the play. Reference to the long line of benefactors and powerful aristocrats of whom the real Galilei was a protégé is likewise tactfully omitted. And even a detail like his writing in the vernacular – really a strategy for gaining wider recognition of his ideas – is given an egalitarian twist. Certainly, one would not have heard the real Galilei saying to Andrea 'Ich will gerade, daß auch du es begreifst' (p.11), not just because he is young, but for class reasons; or asking for the dispute to be 'in der Umgangssprache' so that Federzoni the lens-grinder can understand it (p.45); or expressing genuine solidarity with the Campagna peasants. Brecht's Galilei is a John the Baptist of socialism in a way that his real historical counterpart was not. Thus stylized, Brecht's figure helps polarize the conflicts of the time more sharply.

Brecht on the whole displays more fidelity in his presentation of Galilei's scientific work than in his treatment of the general history of the period. If Galilei's *Sidereus Nuncius* appeared in 1610, then Brecht has him, in January of that year (Scene 3), making the discoveries which will find their way into print under this title. The *Discourse on Floating Bodies* of 1612 finds its reflection in the hydrostatic experiment described in Scene 9. This scene, not dated, is referred to as coming after eight years of silence, so the time must be c. 1624. Here Brecht has delayed mention of such work on flotation in order to accentuate the picture of a man turning to other forms of physical experiment when astronomy becomes too dangerous. The *Dialogue on the Two Great World Systems* of 1632, by far the biggest bone of contention between Galilei and the Vatican, plays an integral part in the action. It is on the Shrove Tuesday of the year of its publication that the insurrectionist carnival pageant is set. In Scene 11 this is the book which Galilei tries to present to Cosmo ('Ich wollte Eurer Hoheit meine Dialoge über die beiden größten Weltsysteme...', p.103). But to no avail: he is cut short in mid-attempt; and it is this book which is put on the Index after Galilei's recantation in 1633. In *Leben des Galilei*, one has the impression that it is because of the political unrest the *Dialogue* is fomenting that Galilei is ordered to Rome, not because of the theological objections that the Church has to Galilei's arguments. As Grimm has shown, this part of the play has also been streamlined by a change of date: 'das enge zeitliche Zusammenrücken von der VI. und VII. Szene durch die Falschdatierung des Gutachtens von Christopher Clavius [führt] zu einer starken Straffung der Handlungsabfolge zwischen Bestätigung der Galileischen Beobachtungen und Indizierung der kopernikanischen Lehre' (*14*, p.157). This sense of an increasing polarization of the two camps is reinforced by the skilful positioning of the 1632 carnival scene. The result is an image of the Church feeling more threatened by popular discontent at grass-roots level, resorting to charges of heresy as a pretext to hold down the opposition by means of fear and coercion. This may explain why Brecht makes no reference to the strong faction of scientists marshalled against Galilei under Colombe's leadership. Neither he nor any of Galilei's other scientific adversaries, including Scheiner and Grassi, are allowed to complicate the sense of a collision between science and religion. Brecht also ignores the fact that Giordano Bruno was actually sent to the stake for religious heresy in his other writings, not for his scientific ideas. In *Leben des Galilei*, it looks as if he had to die because he could not prove the theologically unacceptable Copernican hypothesis. There is also no hint in Brecht of the important role the mood of the Counter-Reformation played in Bruno's death and the treatment of Galilei. The conflict is defined as one between oppressive power and the truth, not between various factions warring for academic or theological reasons, or a mixture of both.

The image one has in Scene 14 of Galilei's recantation holding up the progress of scientific investigation across Europe is, however, largely accurate. Descartes did destroy some of his work when he heard the news, and the Counter-Reformation did score many lesser victories throughout the world of learning. Some commentators have objected to this image of one man retarding the entire historical process as being at root an un-Marxist overrating of the individual, possibly at the cost of misrepresenting the supra-personal historical process. But Brecht's aim here is to stress the responsibility of the individual, and he is prepared to play down the image of history as process in order to do so. As Galilei says at one point: 'Es setzt sich nur so viel Wahrheit durch, als wir durchsetzen; der Sieg der Vernunft kann nur der Sieg der Vernünftigen sein' (p.78).

A number of elements in *Leben des Galilei* are more or less pure invention. No plagiarizing of a Dutch telescope took place in the questionable way in which Brecht suggests; all Galilei did was to improve on a poor instrument that was well known in Italy by that time. Galilei also never soldiered on despite being threatened by the plague. The plague scene has been inserted to point out that society is even more dangerous than natural disasters, and to highlight contrasts between Galilei's behaviour here and in the recantation scene. Unlike Sagredo, who really did collaborate with Galilei and is actually named in the *Dialogue*, two of the leading working-class characters in the play, Andrea and Federzoni, are pure invention (as are Ludovico and Virginia); and so too is Galilei's display of ideological solidarity towards them. Both they and the scene with the Little Monk have been inserted to make Galilei into a more socially conscious, left-wing character, just as the telescope and plague scenes and the encounter with Vanni are there to complicate our picture of his inconsistent behaviour.

Brecht would not have seen his imaginative handling of historical detail in *Leben des Galilei* as a betrayal of fact, any more than a 'Modell' was a betrayal of what a photograph could show. His stylization of the available material (largely culled from Emil Wohlwill's two-volume biography of Galilei, 59) brings out the materialist dialectic of history, a construct that sees class conflict leading to improvements, with all problems being ultimately soluble. 'Die Konflikte werden in unseren Stücken noch geraume Zeit in der Hauptsache Klassenkonflikte sein. [...] Meiner Meinung kann alles, was mit Konflikt, Zusammenstoß, Kampf zusammenhängt, ohne materialistische Dialektik keinesfalls behandelt werden', Brecht once wrote (*GW*16, pp.926f.). In this sense, even though he selects, manipulates and reinterprets the details of Galilei's life and times, he remains true to his Marxist understanding of the historical process and to his agitational aim as a dramatist.

'Als ich *Das Kapital* von Marx las, verstand ich meine Stücke', Brecht confessed in a short piece of the late 1920s entitled 'Der einzige Zuschauer für meine Stücke'. 'Dieser Marx war der einzige Zuschauer für meine Stücke, den ich je gesehen hatte. Denn einen Mann mit solchen Interessen mußten gerade diese Stücke interessieren. Nicht wegen ihrer Intelligenz, sondern wegen der seinigen. Es war Anschauungsmaterial für ihn' (*GW*15, p.129). By the time of *Leben des Galilei*, the 'Anschauungsmaterial' had become even more thoroughly Marxist than anything Brecht had written in the 1920s. Not only in its presentation of the dialectical process, but also in its stress on the materialist nature of historical conflict and in the way it depicted the importance of historical conditioning factors in human behaviour.

4. Epic Structure and Forms of Verfremdung in Leben des Galilei

'Episches Theater', the term favoured by Brecht to launch his new approach to the stage in the late 1920s, possesses a number of interrelated connotations. It began life with largely structural associations. The proposed 'epische Form des Theaters' was from the outset presented as essentially episodic or 'diskontinuierlich': as Brecht said of his plays, 'das einheitliche Ganze besteht aus selbständigen Teilen' (*GW*16, p.655). 'Epic' works therefore tend not to be organized into acts, but consist of a series of smaller, quasi-autonomous parts, with 'Jede Szene für sich' (*GW*17, p.1010). A comparison of *Leben des Galilei* with any classical drama by Racine or Schiller would show that a loose discontinuous series of 'Brechtian' scenes functions in a less emotion-charged way. Brecht summed up Dramatic Theatre (epitomized by the classical five-act play) as having 'eine Szene für die andere' (ibid.), thus contributing to the overall cumulative effect of organic form. With its 'Aufeinandergewiesensein der einzelnen Teile' (*GW*15, p.263), such theatre was, according to Brecht, characterized by 'Wachstum' and 'Zentralisation' rather than the new 'Montage'. The constituent parts of Epic Theatre, by contrast, are more self-contained and closer to compartmentalized mini-dramas. Yet as Brecht's *Kleines Organon für das Theater* acknowledges, there is nothing new to such a conception of epic structure. Goethe and Schiller defined the epic/dramatic contrast in their *Briefwechsel* of April 1797; epic shape had already been a feature of much Shakespearean and Sturm und Drang theatre, and in more recent times Büchner, Strindberg and various German Expressionists had experimented with similarly discontinuous forms. Brecht was simply gearing a pre-existent structural possibility to a new, politically desirable audience response.

Some early theoretical pronouncements give the impression that 'epic' is a term favoured by Brecht (before he hit upon *Verfremdung*) merely to suggest a theatre of distance. With this second connotation, 'episches Theater' refers to a form of audience-response rather than a particular scene-based organization, even if one is to some extent a corollary of the other. The kind of *Dramatic* Theatre to which Brecht was opposed encouraged audience empathy ('Einfühlung') with the central character on stage and discouraged criticism. It derived much of its impact from the immediacy of events seemingly happening as we eavesdrop. We are kept in a state of suspense and emotional involvement mainly because we know little more about what will happen later than do the characters themselves. Brecht dismissed such works as 'kulinarisch' for their pandering to the audience's primitive tastes and unproductive wish to indulge in emotional effects. They were, because of such appeal, inevitably predisposed to reinforce the political *status quo.* Epic Theatre, conceived as an antidote to such affirmative drama, tends to create a very different reponse. As the 'Anmerkungen zur Oper *Mahagonny*' put it, in Dramatic Theatre 'der Zuschauer wird in eine Handlung hineinverversetzt' (a condition unlikely to facilitate critical reaction), whereas 'er wird ihr gegenübergesetzt' (*GW*17, p.1009) in Epic Theatre. Nevertheless, Brecht could be charged with making things too easy for himself by presuming that aesthetic distance would invariably modulate into *critical* distance. Only once (in his *Kleines Organon zum Theater*) do we hear him conceding that epic distance can only be 'der Beginn der Kritik' (*GW*16, p.679).

One could say, figuratively, that the action time of Dramatic Theatre is the present. Sitting in the auditorium, we have a sense of watching things as they occur. Epic Theatre, on the other hand, sets out to deflect attention back to what has already happened; or it treats its material with the kind of distance that the passage of time gives past events, an anteriority which is liable to establish further (intellectual) distance. 'Episches Theater' may thus be associated with the epic genre's retrospection on previous events and, viewed grammatically, with the preterite tense.

The third association of the term is more diffuse, especially when it comes to the devices involved. Semantically, it derives from the link between the idea of an epic quality and the narrative mode (in the German: 'Epik'). In contrast to Dramatic Theatre, which Brecht uncontroversially summed up as 'handelnd', the epic form is conceived as 'erzählend', in that it is more dependent on verbalization than action (*GW*17, p.1009). It displaces the predominance of 'Handlung' with reflection on what has already happened. To this end, it resorts to a vast arsenal of commenting devices.

Not surprisingly, *Leben des Galilei* reveals a predilection for postmortems, retrospective accounts and strategically placed recapitulations. Thus, the momentous encounter between Galilei and the Inquisition, which would have been the centrepiece of a conventional dramatization, takes place off stage, necessitating a plethora of reporting and speculative elements that would have been redundant if it had happened in our presence. More importantly, though not without a measure of exhibited melodrama, the episode remains subservient in length and significance to the ensuing discussion scene assessing the recantation's historical and ethical significance. Scene 14, a more serious 'trial' than the one before the Inquisition, is a prime example of the 'erzählendes Element' which Brecht's theatre privileges.

Of course, a play which traverses whole decades, is consecutively set in three very different political systems (the Venetian Republic, the Tuscan Archduchy and papal Rome), and requires a cast of over thirty named figures and dozens of extras, merits the epithet 'epic', even in the conventional panoramic sense of the word. But as Brecht's theory indicates, *Leben des Galilei* is epic in more than this quantitative sense. It is also so at all levels of the way it tackles its material. Volker Klotz (*50*) has shown how one of the principal differences between dramatic ('closed') and epic ('open') theatre is that the issues raised by the former are in due course contained. A predicament is identified, a contrived intrigue then twists it this way and that, only to solve it by the end of Act Five, with all anti-social behaviour corrected and the threats to society disposed of. 'Open' drama, by contrast, offers a wide-ranging picture of society and its discontents, something to which the appropriate response can only be large-scale social change, rather than the tailor-made aesthetic solution one expects at the end of a traditional play. Usually, these two kinds of theatre diverge in their beginnings as well as their endings. An epic work, because it is not focused on one tragically flawed character or some circumscribed intrigue, will more often than not begin with a less finite *Problemstellung*. Characteristically, we are not treated to a conventional exposition at the start of *Leben des Galilei*. Scene 1 may acquaint us with certain symptomatic aspects of Galilei's behaviour and the context within which he is obliged to work, but it is scarcely more expository than many later episodes. The Naturalist Gerhart Hauptmann once expressed his desire to write a work which was exposition from beginning to end – sheer unfolding of the predicament without resolution or revolution. A play that is all exposition is not obliged to employ its early scenes to set out the kind of problem which can be confronted and solved in due course. Whereas the dilemma has usually been contained when the curtain descends on a closed play, the remark in the epilogue to Brecht's *Der gute Mensch von Sezuan* (that we see 'Den Vorhang zu und alle Fragen offen', *GW*4, p.1607) could also apply to the end of *Leben des Galilei*. Although we eventually leave Galilei behind and witness decisive action being taken, Andrea's final heroic deed falls short of being a satisfactory solution to the political and ideological repression, moral inertia and downright capitulation depicted earlier. There can be no dénouement here: such issues remain part of the world's unfinished business, rather than just a play's. *Leben des Galilei* is open-ended as well as open-structured.

'Der Epiker Döblin', Brecht once recalled (referring to a passage in Alfred Döblin's 'Bemerkungen zum Roman', *47*, p.21), 'gab ein vorzügliches Kennzeichen, als er sagte, Epik könne man im Gegensatz zu Dramatik sozusagen mit der Schere in einzelne Teile schneiden, welche durchaus lebensfähig bleiben' (*GW*15, p.263). Döblin's and Brecht's analogy with a worm hits home, but the metaphor risks raising too many expectations. There can be no absolute structural discontinuity in a work of literature. Brecht's play is, as we have seen, primarily concerned with highlighting 'kausale Zusammenhänge' between behaviour and conditioning factors, so in this respect there cannot but be an integrating cause-and-effect pattern linking various scenes. If Galilei had not been enjoined to produce money-spinning discoveries, he would not have 'rendered unto Caesar' his telescope in Scene 2; had he not felt disadvantaged by conditions in the Venetian Republic, he would not have risked the move to Florence. Subsequent scenes are very much bound together in their illustrative concern with his discoveries and their social implications, yet we at the same time register a threat building up from scene to scene as Galilei progressively underestimates the power of the Church and the Establishment's imperviousness to reasoned argument. Most scenes could scarcely be shuffled and presented in an alternative order. *Leben des Galilei* in fact represents a complex amalgam of discontinuous and concatenating features. Emotional energy may be prevented from spilling over too drastically from one scene into the next by having individual scenes centre on local subplots and relatively self-contained controversies. But the play still displays a distinct teleology as it works towards Galilei's recantation and the exploration of its significance.

A further limit to the autonomy of parts comes from the way in which scenes form thematic or chronological clusters. The early ones are bound together by dint of being set in the Venetian Republic and serving to document how exploited Galilei is. Later comes a more discontinuous series of scenes set in Tuscany, some concerned with the new astronomical discoveries and their reception, others with Galilei's private life, but all preparing the ground for his ultimate silencing. The uneven passage of time serves to create further sub-groupings of scenes, with the first three all being set at approximately the same time, just as the scenes leading up to the recantation occur within one year. By contrast, there is a much greater hiatus between Scene 13 and the meeting between Andrea and Galilei, with the final scene following on directly as the positive consequence of their discussion. There are, contrary to the theory, substructures to the play's overall epic disposition. There have even been attempts (9) to trip Brecht up by positing the pattern of an old-fashioned five-act play underlying the entire work. If this were so (and the evidence is tenuous), it would represent a strange betrayal of aesthetic principle on the author's part, for a purpose which would be difficult to fathom.

One further respect in which *Leben des Galilei* is less radically epic than, say, *Der kaukasische Kreidekreis* lies in the way in which it chronicles the life of one central figure, thereby risking the danger – one Brecht encountered in the case of Mutter Courage – of audiences identifying uncritically with a character as a result of having invested so much interest in him or her for scene after scene. To be sure, Galilei occasionally absents himself, but he is invariably still there as a powerful looming presence. Being perilously close to the centripency of dramatized biography, the work has to bring other techniques to bear to create critical distance vis-à-vis the protagonist. Hence, the marked discontinuity to the quality of his appearances. The Galilei whom we hear theorizing in Scene 14 is no longer the person we encountered in the previous scene: having thought things through, he has shifted his ground radically. Even the Galilei of Scene 13 was so broken when he came on stage that he hardly resembled the man we remember from before: '*völlig, beinahe bis zur Unkenntlichkeit verändert durch den Prozeß*' (p.113), he is a *Verfremdung* of his former self. Even the Andrea of Scene 14 differs markedly from the person we last saw raging against his earlier mentor; and Virginia, now a 'Spitzel der Inquisition', has become a far more frightening figure than she was before. With people changing in the gaps between scenes, a certain montage quality is created. Figures may not be as artificially polarized as the Shen Te and Shui Ta of *Der gute Mensch von Sezuan*, but the many discontinuities to their presentation still contribute to the 'epic' quality of the play.

Various further infrastructures also establish cross-connexions between the individual scenes and militate against any simple autonomy of parts. One of Brecht's theses in 'Dialektik und Verfremdung' reads: 'Das eine verstanden durch das andere (die Szene, im Sinn zunächst selbständig, wird durch ihren Zusammenhang mit andern Szenen noch als eines andern Sinns teilhaftig entdeckt)' (*GW*15, p.361). An unobjectionable hermeneutic principle, one might think, but this means that different parts of a work, far from being received in isolation, acquire meaning as part of a complex.

In practice what we often encounter is a series of antithetical pairs of scenes. Drafts reveal that Brecht planned *Leben des Galilei* very much as a series of contrasting incidents. For instance: 'Er widersteht der Pest, er widersteht nicht der Inquisition' (*34*, p.285). Sometimes, these work plans invite the suspicion that Brecht could become fascinated by an ingenious play with antitheses simply for its own sake. Notes for the American version (with its twelve scenes) at times betray a manneristic playfulness:

> there is morning in 1), and evening in 12)
> there is a gift of an astronomical model in 1), of a goose in 12)
> there is an (astronomical) lecture for Andrea, the boy in 1)
> and a (social) lecture for Andrea, the man in 12) (*34*, p.286)

There are *two* carnivals in the play. In the one, the 'Obrigkeit' take their pleasures at the same time as intimidating Galilei; in the other, the people exalt at their new-found sense of freedom and lionize him as their potential champion. The one 'carnival' is concerned with suppressing truth, the other with disseminating it. In Scene 2, Galilei enjoys a short-lived success with his lies about the telescope to the people of Venice, whereas in Scene 4 he fails to convince Cosmo and his courtiers of the truth (again with a telescope). Galilei's remarks to Mucius in one scene are directed against him later, when he has become a second Mucius. Scenes in which Galilei betrays a fatherly interest in Andrea contrast with moments of callousness towards his daughter. Those where he shows scientific circumspection contrast with his social myopia in others, thus illustrating Sagredo's verdict: 'So mißtrauisch in deiner Wissenschaft, bist du leichtgläubig wie ein Kind in allem, was dir ihr Betreiben zu erleichtern scheint. Du glaubst nicht an den Aristoteles, aber an den Großherzog von Florenz' (p.39). According to eyewitnesses, 'Brecht hat in den Proben wiederholt auf die antithetischen Züge in der Komposition hingewiesen; *aber er betonte meistens sofort den dialektischen*

Zusammenhang' (*34*, p.248, my emphasis). But such patterns do not always lead to productive insights, all antitheses do not a dialectic make.

The most challenging contrast is that between the man who risks his life to continue working during the plague and yet recants before the Inquisition. Even the structural device of having a Section (a) and a Section (b) to the plague scene (juxtaposing the others' headlong rush to escape with Galilei's bravely staying on to work) underlines this paradox. Why does he not behave like most of the rest of his household and save his skin (as he will in Scene 13)? There is no one unequivocal explanation. In the plague scene, Galilei is on the brink of completing 'Aufzeichnungen von drei Monaten, die ich wegschmeißen kann, wenn ich sie nicht noch ein, zwei Nächte fortführe' (p.52). Later, however, with 'alle Beweise zusammen' (p.57), nothing can jeopardize them, even if he personally can still be muzzled. An alternative reading is that, unlike the instruments of torture, the plague is too abstract a threat to intimidate this 'Mann des Fleisches'. But a further factor may not be irrelevant to the differences between the two scenes.

In his encounter with Mucius, Galilei refers to the threat from the plague as 'keine Kleinigkeit' (p.52). 'Sagen Sie nichts von Schwierigkeiten! Ich habe mich von der Pest nicht abhalten lassen, meine Notierungen fortzusetzen.' In response to which he is told: 'die Pest ist nicht das Schlimmste' (p.81). Mucius is on the right track. Of the two threats mentioned as far back as Scene 1 ('Aberglauben und Pest' (p.8)), a reactionary society represents by far the greater danger. When talking about fatalism, Brecht frequently juxtaposes attitudes to natural disasters and to man-made problems: 'So werden sie fertig mit den Erdbeben und nicht mit ihresgleichen selber' (*GW*16, p.525). The contrast between Scene 5 and Scene 13 may make the audience recognize that social threats are more destructive than the natural disasters with which they are often equated.

The constituent scenes of *Leben des Galilei* cannot, also for other reasons, be viewed as fifteen equal components. Some are more distancing than others. Revealingly, in 1938, the scene between Galilei and the Little Monk stood out as an exception in being unnumbered. It was simply entitled 'Verwandlung' (*BFA*5, p.64): a reference to the way Galilei wins the monk over, and thus a sharp contrast to the way in which the Pope is later going to be metamorphosed in the other direction to become a tool of the powers that be. ('Verwandlung' is also the title of a later scene (*BFA*5, pp.88ff.) where the Church authorities rebuff Galilei.) The scene with the monk stands outside and above the main action of the play, offering a general discussion of underlying issues. One litmus test of its 'epic' commenting status lies in the fact that it could be inserted at any number of points without detriment to its function. Brecht did later number it, but the fact remains that this and certain other scenes are not part of any ongoing action, but act instead as comment. Hence, epic structure is not only a matter of linear discontinuity but of individual scenes serving different kinds of function. Helmut Jendreiek has argued that the play's organization operates on two levels: 'auf der Ebene des dramatischen Vorgangs und der Ebene philosophischer Reflexion' (*20*, p.290). Indeed, this *Nebeneinander* of action and reflection occurs not only in the different status of individual scenes but within scenes.

One of the striking features of the American version of the play was the way in which each individual scene was divided into sub-units by the use of section titles. Scene 1, for example, consisted of five main components or mini-scenes:

1. THE BOY, ANDREA SARTI, WHEEDLES A FREE LESSON FROM THE GREAT GALILEO BY BEING INTERESTED.
2. WHILE HAVING HIS BACK RUBBED, GALILEO ANNOUNCES A NEW AGE.
3. IN STRAITENED CIRCUMSTANCES THE GREAT PHYSICIST HAS TO TAKE A WEALTHY PUPIL INSTEAD OF AN INTELLIGENT ONE.
4. GALILEO PLEADS FOR LEISURE TO PROVE HIS HYPOTHESES; THE UNIVERSITY AUTHORITIES DEMAND COMMERCIAL INVENTIONS.
5. HAVING HEARD OF A NEW DUTCH INSTRUMENT, GALILEO TO GET MONEY BUILDS A TELESCOPE. (*BFA*5, pp.119-25)

It is tempting to speculate about the grounds for including these headings and for their later removal. It may not be immaterial that they were inserted at a time when Brecht was emerging from adverse experiences with the Zurich production of *Mutter Courage und ihre Kinder*. By the 1950s, it is possible that headings of this kind had become such a conventionalized aspect of a 'Brechtian' production that the playwright judged them to have become too predictable and unable to carry out their defamiliarizing task. In any case, the epic substructures to which these headings draw attention remain. Indeed, epic structure is detectable not just in the fragmented character of each individual scene, it permeates into the syntax of individual sentences, with their predilection for parenthetic insertions, parallelisms, phrases in apposition and parataxis; and it is a product of the rapid changes of mood that characterize *Leben des Galilei*.

In his exploration of the play's two-level structure, Jendreiek (*20*, pp.291-93) itemizes a whole series of passages offering 'sentenziöse Zusammenfassungen der im Stückvorgang diskutierten Ansichten', episodes which not so much advance the course of the action as amplify its significance. Scene 1's hymn to the new age is one; so too are the discussion with the Little Monk, the act of self-criticism in Scene 14 and a number of smaller passages which seem to interrupt the action by soaring into an elevated register ('rhythmisierte Prosa', to use Jendreiek's term (*20*, p.293)). One important recapitulatory sequence is sited, not within a scene, but beyond its conclusion. After the devastating news of the recantation has been received by Galilei's followers, the curtain drops leaving the fallen man alone down stage. Changing roles (as the figures of *Die Dreigroschenoper* do to sing their songs), he reads out a passage from his *Discorsi*. The play concludes what is still an emotional scene with an epilogue which allows us to stand back from the immediate impact of Galilei's 'Sündenfall' and ponder its significance. Injecting the scientific terminology of the *Discorsi* into the debate enables us to extricate ourselves from the turmoil of the moment. It offsets the bleakness of a social criminal's capitulation by reminding us that he is going on to write his *magnum opus*; and in tone it contrasts with the disappointed Andrea's outburst by showing us the measured prose of a later Galilei at his intellectual peak.

Although this postscript was only added in the 1950s, the imagery generated by some of Galilei's earlier experiments had already given the audience a series of frameworks within which to view the protagonist's behaviour (although whether one sees them as *epic* distancing or *Verfremdung* may simply be a matter of personal choice). In particular, the detailed description of Galilei's experiments with floating bodies in Scene 9 offers a dramatized equivalent to Scene 13's epilogue; it is certainly there to provide more than just a snapshot of the discoverer at work. Like the image of falling which Scene 13's conclusion employs as an analogy for social behaviour, the flotation experiment offers a *Modell* for the interpretation of human actions. Although the scene communicates the care and precision with which Galilei sets up an experiment, such a sense of meticulous work procedures had already been established in Scene 3; moreover, the point that Galilei has been forced to discontinue his main astronomical work could have been put over in a couple of lines. The true import of this episode lies in the interpretive imagery it presents. The object is to discover what laws govern floating bodies ('Körper', audiences will need no reminding, is a word very much associated with Galilei's physical presence from Scene 1 onwards). Galilei and his assistants set out to ascertain what has to happen so that a body – any body, anybody, but specifically the corpulent hero – will float or go under.

Surprisingly, the episode ends before any result has been reached. The real Galilei proved that a body sinks if it weighs more than the water it displaces, whereas if it is lighter, it floats. He thus demolished the contemporary assumption, championed by his rival Colombe, that it was primarily shape that determined what floated. Galilei arrived at his findings on the basis of a series of complex experiments involving wax and lead shot. Obviously, Brecht would have had difficulty reflecting the intricacies of all this on stage, but he appears to go to the opposite extreme by having his hero arrive at no conclusive result at all. The investigation is interrupted in its preliminary stages by an exchange between Galilei and Mucius, who is castigated for having betrayed his scientific integrity, in other words for having 'sunk' or 'fallen'. Galilei's most scathing remark

('Wer die Wahrheit nicht weiß, der ist bloß ein Dummkopf. Aber wer sie weiß und sie eine Lüge nennt, der ist ein Verbrecher!', p.81) thus comes in the context of an investigation into what factors cause objects to sink. When in Scene 13 we come back to these specific words, we are presumably meant to recall the imagery of floating (or sinking) associated with the time when they were first heard.

One thing that the flotation experiment and the *Discorsi* quotation have in common is the way they confront us with unanswered questions. By not being concluded, the investigation in Scene 9 leaves it to us to ascertain just what factors do cause things – and people – to float or sink. The passage from the *Discorsi* (Brecht doctored the original for this purpose) asks about how the laws of gravitation relate to different categories of subject. The implication is that 'Größe' (a play on 'size' and 'greatness') is an operative factor. But the emphases of the two analogies remain different. Whereas the experiment with *floating* bodies stresses the image of rising to the surface, something that Galilei is still trying to do at this stage, the *Discorsi* passage concentrates, more appropriately by then, on the destruction that results from the *falling* of large bodies, as well as introducing the question of whether or not there are special cases. We also find a distinction in the scientific passage between what happens to large and small falling objects. Yet this may be intended more as a provocation than an insight, for although size has an effect on the repercussions of a fall, bodies of all size are still subject to the general laws of gravitation. It would be surprising to find a special case being made out for Galilei by these epic insertions. If Galilei's story illustrates the 'Gesetzlichkeiten, die sein Leben beherrschen' (*16*, p.52), these are largely principles of *Entfremdung* (in Marx's sense) operating right across the society in which he lives.

As we turn now from some of the *epic* features of Brecht's play to view the work as *Verfremdungstheater*, some indication of the relationship between the two terms is called for. One of the difficulties with Brecht's theoretical utterances is that their rhetoric makes for inexact terminology. The various labels used to identify the theatre he adamantly opposes ('Dramatische Form des Theaters', 'Aristotelisches Theater', 'kulinarisches Theater', 'Einfühlungstheater',

'Illusionismus') have different associations, although they overlap to
some degree. The same is true of the terms 'Episches Theater' and
'Verfremdung'.

In 'Einige Irrtümer über die Spielweise des Berliner Ensembles'
Brecht defined estrangement's aim in the following terms: 'daß man
auf der Bühne nichts "selbstverständlich" sein läßt' (*GW*16, p.910).
According to 'Vergnügungstheater oder Lehrtheater?': 'Von keiner
Seite wurde es dem Zuschauer weiterhin ermöglicht, durch einfache
Einfühlung in dramatische Personen sich kritiklos (und praktisch
folgenlos) Erlebnissen hinzugeben' (*GW*15, pp.264f.). Inasmuch as
'Episches Theater' had been conceived of as a theatre of critical
distance, it shares that goal with *Verfremdung* (which means 'making
strange' or 'defamiliarizing' something, not *alienating the audience*,
as some misguided interpretations would have it). It may therefore
help to think of 'Episches Theater' and 'Verfremdung' as two
strategies – one largely structural or 'erzählend', the other involving
various forms of stylization – with essentially the same purpose, epic
discontinuity being continually reinforced by a series of estranging
devices. One could even construct a hierarchy of *Verfremdungseffekte*, from large-scale factors like choice of genre (the
predilection for the parable form) or historical and geographical
distancing (or in *Leben des Galilei* an amalgam of both) right down
to single words, gestures and local theatrical signals. Near the apex
would also come the choice of dominant *Verhaltensmuster* and the
way it had been translated into an unfamiliar form: the scientist as a
defamiliarizing presentation of the social obligations of everyone or
Mutter Courage, the 'Marketenderin', as a rejection of the cliché
image of the capitalist, so that we can now focus more on the
underlying mentality. 'Warum ist die negative Hauptperson so viel
interessanter als der positive Held?' Brecht once asked. His answer:
'Sie wird kritisch dargestellt' (*GW*16, p.918). The choice of central
figure is a much underestimated form of *Verfremdungseffekt* (simply
because Brecht seldom theorized on the subject), although as we saw
in Chapter 2, the central figure's contradictions can dominate a play.

'Eine verfremdende Abbildung ist eine solche, die den
Gegenstand zwar erkennen, ihn aber doch zugleich fremd erscheinen

läßt' (*GW*16, p.680). Some strategies which effect this complex process of both making recognizable and yet offering a series of controlled 'Verfremdungen des Vertrauten' (*GW*16, p.682) operate at a high level of generality. Further down the scale come a series of devices intended to make things we do not normally question suddenly appear in a new light, or local, artificial devices to make sure that we realize we are in the theatre watching a play, not observing real-life events happening. 'Es handelt sich [...] um eine Technik, mit der darzustellenden Vorgängen zwischen Menschen der Stempel des Auffallenden, des der Erklärung Bedürftigen, nicht Selbstverständlichen, nicht einfach Natürlichen verliehen werden kann. Der Zweck des Effekts ist, dem Zuschauer eine fruchtbare Kritik vom gesellschaftlichen Standpunkt aus zu ermöglichen' (*GW*16, p.553). An account of *Verfremdung* which did not relate it to its political function would be too narrow, given that 'die echten V-Effekte haben kämpferischen Charakter' (*GW*16, p.706). Admittedly, many such devices do also have a cognitive function ('Das "Natürliche" mußte das Moment des *Auffälligen* bekommen. Nur so konnten die Gesetze von Ursache und Wirkung zutage treten', *GW*15, p.265). But new insight is only important inasmuch as it leads to corrective action. Hence, part of Brecht's conception of the device is that it should only be applied to the depiction of phenomena capable of being changed: 'Die neuen Verfremdungen sollten nur den gesellschaftlich beeinflußbaren Vorgängen den Stempel des Vertrauten wegnehmen, der sie heute vor dem Eingriff bewahrt' (*GW*16, p.681).

To take a simple example: Galilei's phrase 'es ist mir hinaufgefallen' (p.61), in reference to the *Beweisstein* which he has provocatively dropped in front of the Collegium Romanum monks, is calculated to create a new framework of thinking. Notions of 'up' and 'down' were at this time undergoing radical destabilization, both because the Earth was being seen to be round and because its place in the universe was being rethought (which, of course, had implications for the feudal social pyramid). At plot level, Galilei's expression is an example of *Verfremdung*: he is breaking with a normal expression in order to jolt the monks out of their customary thought patterns.

Nevertheless, the most important devices perform more than just an illusion-breaking function, as, for example, when Andreas mispronounces Copernicus as 'Kippernikus' (p.11). This might, in another kind of work, simply have served to underline how young he still is. But given that Brecht's play is going to make a political point about pedantically academic mumbo-jumbo and have Galilei demonstratively holding a disputation in the vernacular for the benefit of those present who do not have Latin, we are obviously meant to see more in this mispronunciation than plausible realism or comedy. Although unable to pronounce Copernicus' name properly, Andrea nevertheless grasps the workings of the heliocentric system far more quickly than many of the scholars we encounter later, people for whom Copernicus' name would not be a tongue-twister. In fact, just one mispronounced word draws attention to two conflicting notions of intelligence: a pedantic scholarly elitist one versus the true open-minded grasp of an issue ('Vernunft', unlike Latin, is not the preserve of the ruling class). In addition, an association of the mistake with the verb 'kippen' may also evoke the overturning of old ideas.

In Scene 15, Brecht employs a comparably neat tactic of estrangement via pantomime to highlight the ruse by which Andrea secretes the *Discorsi* across the border (and it is not 'unter dem Rock' as the previous scene had prophesied; so what we expect and what we see are deliberately contrasted). The stage directions at the beginning of the scene note that Andrea '*sitzt auf einer kleinen Kiste und liest in Galileis Manuskript*' (p.128). So as not to be missed, the point of his subterfuge has to be communicated to the audience by estrangement. '*Die Jungen gehen, um den lesenden Andrea zu verspotten, so herum, als läsen auch sie in Büchern beim Gehen*' (p.129). To ensure we see more than the guards, Brecht shows us both Andrea and a series of caricaturing, duplicate Andreas all engaged in the same activity. The fact that these ignorant children consider the sight of someone reading worthy of ridicule ultimately rebounds on them. Hence, if the device of pantomime shows us the cunning with which what *Die Maßnahme* calls 'illegale Arbeit' has to be carried out, it also offers us a sense of the historical process, as we observe the kind of scorn of education which will one day – and in another kind of society – be a thing of the past.

This is not the only moment where imitation becomes *Verfremdung*. (Indeed, Brecht's theoretical ruminations in 'Die Straßenszene' put a great deal of emphasis on the strategy of repetition, cf. *GW*16, p.548). The encounter between Andrea and Cosmo, where the two boys play the parts of grown-ups ('Hier geht es zu wie in einem Taubenschlag', 'Verstehe', p.41), acts as a distancing prelude to the forthcoming grand dispute. That Andrea is seen to be imitating Galilei will acquire more resonance at the later point where – ethically, at least – he will outstrip his mentor. Similarly, the Collegium Romanum monks' lampooning of what they take to be Galilei's nonsensical opinions at the start of Scene 6 offers a stylized contrast between his discoveries and their *sancta simplicitas*, as the estranging pun calls it. Likewise, 'the way Frau Sarti also risks the plague by staying behind with Galilei acts as a kind of extended displacement of his behaviour, inviting us to compare their motives and see similarities between her addiction to looking after him and his obsession with science (which will be presented as a kind of perversion from which he cannot refrain in Scene 14). Such acts of duplication remain quite plausible at plot level (all forms of *Verfremdung* are by no means radically 'antiillusionistisch'), but this does not prevent them from serving further reflective purposes.

Brecht employs three main types of *Verfremdung*: what he sometimes referred to as *textliche, szenische* and *darstellerische* forms. Two of these, stage-sets and acting methods, will be the topic of the next chapter. My present concern is with forms of estrangement embedded in the language of *Leben des Galilei*. These textual elements are more crucial than anyone reading Brecht's theory would suppose, but that is simply because the theory is mainly concerned with production problems and not with how to write *Verfremdungstheater*.

Many of Brecht's linguistic devices serve an illusion-breaking function. Although there is a tendency to associate *Verfremdung* with new critical insights (a Brechtian version of the Hegelian 'Bekannt ist nicht erkannt'), a considerable proportion of *Verfremdungseffekte* are tactical devices inserted to counteract the emotional propensities of an episode or at least to remind audiences that they are watching a play in the theatre which has been devised to *show* them something. Referring once in a dialogue to what must not happen to an audience in his kind of theatre ('Vielleicht will es [...] vergessen, daß es im Theater ist'), Brecht inserts the remark: 'Das können wir so wenig dulden, wie daß sie vergäßen, daß sie immer noch "im Leben" sind', i.e. when sitting in their theatre seats (*GW*16, p.917). *Verfremdungen* thus also remind us that we are in a theatre, not to switch off, but to learn about the nature of society. Hence, instead of a consistent register of archaic language to create the impression that we are watching something really happening in seventeenth-century Italy, stylistic anachronisms help to break the illusion of duplicated reality that a historical play might risk creating. Scene 1's reference to 'der Milchmann' sounds out of place; it is too modern and suggests a translated American idea. The word 'Blamage' (p.40) draws attention to the fact that Frau Sarti is more worldly and sensible than Galilei in her prediction of how the encounter with Cosmo will end; and the use of 'Kubikmillimeter' (p.49) highlights the fact that our ignorance is virtually infinite and yet it can be reduced by minimal amounts all the time. The Cardinal Inquisitor's reference to 'materielle Interessen' (p.107) alerts us to the fact that his arguments are essentially those of *Machtpolitik* reinforcing the Church's own material interests. It takes modern terminology to diagnose the kind of thinking encountered here.

Words can also puncture the quasi-realistic linguistic continuum without standing out as anachronisms. In Scene 2, at the end of his hypocritical speech about the telescope, Galilei mutters under his breath the one word 'Zeitverlust' (p.24). If there has up until then been any risk of the audience being carried away by all the rhetoric, this will help prevent any such emotional impact. In fact, curtailing 'Einfühlung' is, along with 'Antiillusionismus', one of estrangement's recurrent functions.

It is doubtful whether any device which, because it occurs in Brecht's work, becomes a candidate for the label 'alienation device' is actually a technical innovation. As he recognized, 'Der v-effekt ist ein altes kunstmittel, bekannt aus der komödie, gewissen zweigen der volkskunst und der praxis des asiatischen theaters' (*1*, p.137). *Verfremdung*, in other words, is effected by a conglomerate of redeployed traditional devices – and not only derived from the sources he mentions here. To take two central techniques: quotations and allegorical imagery both belong to literature's stock-in-trade, but here they are inserted in such a way as to function as *Verfremdungseffekte*.

In Scene 1, at the end of his peroration to the New Age, Galilei turns to Andrea and asks 'Wie sagt der Dichter? "O früher Morgen des Beginnens!"', only to be rewarded with the lines:

'O früher Morgen des Beginnens!
O Hauch des Windes, der
Von neuen Küsten kommt!'

The poem acts as a *Verfremdung* of Galilei's earlier words by taking them up on to a more lyrical plane, ultimately only to have them deflated as Andrea interrupts with the words 'Und Sie müssen Ihre Milch trinken, denn dann kommen sofort wieder Leute' (p.10). If we have been too willing to rise on the wings of Galilei's ecstasy up until this point, Andrea has rightly taken him and us down a peg or two. No doubt, we are intended to remember this incident the next time a poem is quoted in the play. Not far into Scene 7 we are told: '*Aus dem Ballsaal hört man* [...] *den Beginn des berühmten Gedichts Lorenzo di Medicis über die Vergänglichkeit*':

'Ich, der ich Rosen aber sterben sah
Und ihre Blätter lagen welkend da
Entfärbt auf kaltem Boden, wußte gut:
Wie eitel ist der Jugend Übermut!' (p.65)

Such images of transitory and misplaced youthful enthusiasm invite us to stand back and see how mistaken and threatened Galilei is at this stage when he is about to be warned by Bellarmin and Barberini. That a poem about transience, commenting on Galilei's precarious situation, is associated with the Medici family is an appropriate detail. It is as if the pessimism of the second poem has cancelled out the exhilaration of the earlier one; though the audience is in fact being confronted with a paradox that requires digestion.

Quotations not only comment on the action of the moment, they can also refer us to other parts of the play. When Galilei is replying to the set of quotations sent to him while he is incarcerated at Arcetri, we are reminded of his earlier battle of quotations with Bellarmin and Barberini. In the first, he radiated confidence of victory, in the later scene we see a weak old man having to respond to chosen passages sent for his edification by the Church and only able to indulge in an occasional irony.

People who quote are, of course, not speaking with their own voice. Sometimes they quote others in order to put their words under the microscope, as when Frau Sarti imitates Galilei at the start of Scene 4. Sometimes their words are thrown back at them by others: for instance, Galilei's sycophantic letter to Cosmo, in part read out during Scene 3 (p.37), is cited in fuller detail at the end (p.39). Given that Sagredo had already objected on the grounds that Cosmo was only nine at the time, the fact that the flattery is even more expansive in the second passage shows Galilei has not taken any notice of his friend's advice. He now stands condemned by his false words. Sometimes we have mock quotations, remarks imputed to people summing up what they could have said (Galilei's phrase 'Besser befleckt als leer', p.122), or the carnival participants attribute revolutionary sentiments to Galilei. Such pseudo-quotations often play the role of Aunt Sallies: remarks invented in order to be attacked. What is clear is that quotation is not resorted to for the purpose of creating a sense of historical authenticity. (Galilei's sycophantic letter to the boy-prince employs forms of seventeenth-century hyperbole appropriate to addressing a noble patron, but we listen to it with twentieth-century ears.) Highlighting an expression or a behaviour pattern, quotation subjects it to scrutiny and suggests that the element is worthy of the audience's suspicion.

Allegory and emblem are also deployed as estranging devices. Repeatedly, issues are exposed as in need of a critical reappraisal by being expressed allegorically. The introductory couplet in Scene 4 highlights the dominant pattern of the episode that follows: 'Das Alte sagt: So wie ich bin, bin ich seit je. / Das Neue sagt: Bist du nicht gut, dann geh' (p.40). Or Scene 13's: 'Aus Finsternis trat die Vernunft herfür / Ein' ganzen Tag stand sie vor der Tür' (p.109). At the moment in Scene 3 where Galilei and Sagredo discover the mountains of the moon, Galilei observes: 'Heute ist der 10. Januar 1610. Die Menschheit trägt in ihr Journal ein: Himmel abgeschafft' (p.28), an essentially allegorical personification, later to be trumped by the suggestion that it is the Pope who will write a comparable entry in his 'Tagebuch' (p.38). Elsewhere Galilei refers to a 'Perlmutterdunst von Aberglauben', and the whole emblem of the oyster (beauty achieved through suffering) is essentially an allegory.

Galilei frequently resorts to bold images to sum up or give impact to some point: '[Es] ist eine Zugluft entstanden, welche sogar den Fürsten und Prälaten die goldbestickten Röcke lüftet, so daß fette und dürre Beine darunter sichtbar werden, Beine wie unsere Beine' (pp.9f.). Such a passage is not far removed from the structure of the baroque emblem with its pairing of image and verbal commentary (*pictura* and *subscriptio*). When Galilei senses the resistance of Barberini to his ideas in Scene 7, he tries to help the man out of his customary thought process by means of a *verfremdende* analogy: 'Als ich [...] klein war [...], Eure Eminenz, stand ich auf einem Schiff, und ich rief: Das Ufer bewegt sich fort. – Heute weiß ich, das Ufer stand fest, und das Schiff bewegte sich fort' (p.66). (The insertion of 'Eure Eminenz' at this juncture is a further distancing element, since it ironically introduces a false note of reverence at the very moment when Galilei is equating Barberini's mistaken assumption with that of a young child.)

When Andrea asks Galilei in Scene 1 what a hypothesis is, he is given a neat reformulation of the idea: 'Daß die Felice dort unten, vor dem Korbmacherladen, die ihr Kind an der Brust hat, dem Kind Milch gibt und nicht etwa Milch von ihm empfängt, das ist so lange eine Hypothese, als man nicht hingehen und es sehen und beweisen kann' (p.21). With this defamiliarizing version of the issue firmly established, Galilei is able to turn, confident of getting his ideas

across, to those astronomical advantages which he thinks make all
the difference between himself and Giordano Bruno who was, he
naively assumes, burnt at the stake for offering hypotheses rather
than demonstrable facts.

The geometric truth expressed right at the beginning of the
play, that a straight line is the shortest way between two points (p.7),
seems no more than a truism. But when Andrea tries to gloss Galilei's
recantation favourably in Scene 14, it is reused as a *Verfremdung* of
his behaviour. For the remark 'Angesichts von Hindernissen mag die
kürzeste Linie zwischen zwei Punkten die krumme sein' (p.123) now
gives us a cognitive ethical model with which to try to put a more
charitable gloss on what happened in the previous scene. Imagery of
this kind needs to be particularly striking because it forms part of a
chain of allusions to other parts of the play which must come together
in the audience's mind. When Barberini reminds Galilei of the legend
about the founding of Rome – 'Zwei Knäblein, so geht die Mär,
empfingen Milch und Zuflucht von einer Wölfin. Von der Stunde an
müssen alle Kinder der Wölfin für ihre Milch zahlen. Aber dafür
sorgt die Wölfin für alle Arten von Gemüsen, himmlische und
irdische' (p.67) – the remark comes as the overture to an offer of a
bribe of access to courtesans 'von internationalem Ruf', if Galilei
agrees to be compliant. But we are also meant to notice that Scene 1's
image of paying the milkman has now been metamorphosed into a
version of rendering unto Caesar what is Caesar's coupled with being
offered reciprocal rewards of an enticing kind – by Rome,
represented by the legendary wolf (*lupa* is also Latin for prostitute)
and Rome, in the sense of the all-powerful Church.

If bold imagery facilitates critical distance or affords
contextual insights, we have reached the point where it would not be
unrealistic to view the greater proportion of Brecht's language as a
series of *Verfremdungseffekte*, since anything that supplies a fresh set
of analogies with which to interpret events leads to critical distance.
The Latinate vocabulary and cumbersome syntax of an academic
(p.46), Galilei's meticulous formulations of his scientific programme
in Scene 9 (esp. p.93) or his imagery at the end of the long speech in
Scene 14 ('Eine Menschheit, stolpernd in diesem tausendjährigen

Perlmutterdunst von Aberglauben und alten Wörtern [...] ein Geschlecht erfinderischer Zwerge, die für alles gemietet werden können', pp.125f.), all highlight events and subject them to renewed appraisal. Moreover, the first part of the compound 'Perlmutterdunst' will make us recall what Galilei said about the pearl and the oyster in his conversation with the Little Monk some scenes earlier: 'Zum Teufel mit der Perle, ich ziehe die gesunde Auster vor' (p.77), and his arguments for saying this.

On what is potentially a more circumscribed, realistic plane, correctives arising out of situations where people say something wrong and need to be put in their place, represent an important dialectical form of alienation, since they ensure that we re-examine our attitude to what has just been said. 'Besser befleckt als leer' (p.122) has to be shown to be a misinterpretation of the recantation's rationale. 'Unglücklich das Land, das keine Helden hat' (p.113) invites the rejoinder 'Nein. Unglücklich das Land, das Helden nötig hat' (p.114). When 'göttliche Geduld' is displayed, Galilei feels compelled to ask where people's 'göttlicher Zorn' is skulking (p.79).

Given that *textliche Verfremdung* often entails taking familiar utterances and questioning their underlying assumptions, it is hardly surprising that wordplays and puns are frequently used for this purpose. When Ludovico says 'Die Mutter wünschte, daß ich mich ein wenig umsähe, was in der Welt sich zuträgt usw.', he is already expressing himself in a form that estranges: the subjunctive and the use of 'usw.' suggest an idle rich son forced to obey his mother in order to secure his inheritance. But Galilei's retort, playing on the verb 'sich zutragen' with 'Und Sie hörten in Holland, daß in Italien zum Beispiel ich mich zutrage?' (p.14), makes it clear that we should not be taken in by the spirit in which this prospective pupil is approaching him. He is not seeking knowledge, but simply obeying his mother out of economic prudence. The Kurator's bon mot 'Wozu neue Fallgesetze, wenn nur die Gesetze des Fußfalls wichtig sind?' (p.19) is at least refreshingly honest in its intimidating suggestion that fear of someone coming to take you away is going to override any innocent pride in new scientific discoveries. Scene 4's play on the words 'Staatsball' (for which Cosmo and his courtiers are soon leaving) and 'Eiertanz' (the word the Mathematician uses to suggest that Galilei is being treated too leniently, p.50) draws further attention to the play's elaborate contrast between courtliness and intimidation. Elsewhere, when a book arrives, dedicated to 'Der größten lebenden Autorität in der Physik, Galileo Galilei' (p.83), we recall Galilei's earlier cautionary remarks about the status of authority (p.49); and we may even wonder how long he will remain the greatest *living* authority in his field, if he carries on being a fly in the ecclesiastical ointment.

Traditional irony is also deployed as an estranging effect. When we hear of the Papal Astronomer 'Er sitzt drinnen und glotzt durch dieses Teufelsrohr!' (p.60), Scene 1's distinction between 'Glotzen' and 'Sehen' (p.11) will alert us to the wrong thinking here. If Clavius had been doing no more than 'gawking', then the telescope might still have remained an instrument of the devil in the eyes of those eagerly awaiting a dismissive verdict. If, as turns out to be the case, he is examining it intelligently, the telescope will no longer seem 'dämonisch'. Quite clearly, the compound 'Teufelsrohr' tells us a lot about the Church's fears and its primitive methods of allaying them. Elsewhere, sarcasm backfires as it is subjected to irony: for example, the Philosopher's parting shot in Scene 4, 'Nach allem, was wir hier gehört haben, zweifle ich nicht länger, daß Herr Galilei in den Schiffswerften Bewunderer finden wird' (p.50). To suggest he has followers in such quarters is patently just about the most insulting state of affairs Galilei's adversary can contemplate. But the truth is that for Brecht's Galilei such a situation would be more than flattering. After dictating his commentary to a biblical quotation sent for his attention by the local archbishop, Galilei turns to Virginia with the words: 'Du meinst nicht, daß eine Ironie hineingelesen werden könnte?' (p.117), the point being that irony is invariably an undermining of ostensible meaning. In this case, the ambiguity of the situation rebounds on both Galilei and Virginia: on her, because she cannot see that he is actually being ironic while expressing the hope that no irony will be read into his comments, on him in that irony can represent no more than a pyrrhic victory for someone in his predicament.

There are moments during the Shrove Tuesday Carnival when one aspect of *Verfremdung's* pedigree is made explicit. For many of the ballad-singer's rhymes (i.e. *Volkskunst*) give pause for reflection. When the line 'Auf stund der Doktor Galilei' (possibly containing a pun on the word 'Aufstand') is rhymed with 'die creatio dei' (p.95), there is a whiff of heresy in the air. But when God Himself (in the genitive: 'dei') is then rhymed with the exclamation 'he!', any sense of irreverent provocation is compounded. Comic rhymes become estranging rhymes and hence illuminating ones. The pattern continues. 'Meister' is rhymed with 'dreister' (which is what the underdogs are becoming) and 'dann beißt er' (another 'Vorgeschmack der Zukunft'); 'Meß' (i.e. 'die Messe') is paired with 'keß' (as the faithful get out of line); 'Ach und Weh' (Man's lot) is rhymed with 'Doktor Galuleh' who, it is hoped, will teach people 'Des Erdenglückes großes ABC' (p.97).

The carnival scene is not the only context in which comic rhymes are used for *Verfremdung*. Many of the verses prefacing the individual scenes also operate similarly:

> Groß ist nicht alles, was ein großer Mann tut
> Und Galilei aß gern gut.
> Nun hört, und seid nicht grimm darob
> Die Wahrheit übers Teleskop. (p.23)

At only one juncture are these prefatory couplets not rhymed, and that is Scene 13, where the recantation requires a far darker mood (hence, omitting rhyme becomes an internal *Verfremdung* of the method used elsewhere).

Another form of distancing is produced by the flaunted lapidary phrase. Galilei frequently tosses off sententious remarks so strikingly formulated as to make them memorable in their entirety: 'Die Städte sind eng, und so sind die Köpfe' (p.8); 'Die Wahrheit ist das Kind der Zeit, nicht der Autorität' (p.49); 'Es setzt sich nur so viel Wahrheit durch, als wir durchsetzen; der Sieg der Vernunft kann nur der Sieg der Vernünftigen sein' (p.78). Not all such phrases come from Galilei despite his distinct knack for them. 'Verschissen ist nicht zerrissen', for instance, comes in the song the children sing at the start of Scene 15 (p.128). Usually, the mnemonic factor is crucial because a phrase will be echoed later on, as we saw with the phrase 'Unglücklich das Land, das keine Helden hat!' (p.113). As Brecht puts it in 'Literarisierung des Theaters', 'Auch in die Dramatik ist die Fußnote und das vergleichende Blättern einzuführen' (*GW*17, p.992). Cross-references of this kind become easier to register, if the first instance is memorably formulated.

What emerges, from even this small selection of examples, is just how great the range of verbal distancing techniques is and what a spectrum of purposes *Verfremdung* serves.

In later years, Brecht criticized the terms *Episches Theater* and *Verfremdung* as 'zu formal' (*GW*16, p.869). His eventual preferred concept was 'Dialektisches Theater'. But as Schumacher demonstrates, Brecht was writing Dialectical Theatre *avant la lettre* long before he considered this the best consolidating label for his method. One of the new term's attractions was the way it brought his work more into line with orthodox Marxist aesthetics. But the concept also stressed the coming together of dialectical content (including contradictions in the individual's behaviour and images of history as class struggle) and the effect Brecht wished to have on his audiences. For any estranging device is ultimately dialectical in effect. It takes the familiar (as its thesis) and estranges it (by suggesting the antithesis), a process encouraging the audience to push forward to a synthesizing understanding of why 'das Natürliche' has been deliberately made to look strange. A response involving critical distance rather than empathy is necessarily a dialectical one, for what the characters are doing or saying on stage becomes a thesis to which we must construct an antithesis (the 'Nicht-Sondern' model, as Brecht calls it (*GW*16, p.688)): 'das Publikum [dichtet] im Geist andere Verhaltungsweisen und Situationen hinzu und hält sie [...] gegen die vom Theater vorgebrachten' (*GW*16, p.924). As this stress on audience response implies, the impact of *Leben des Galilei* lies not on the page, but is a result of being effectively staged. 'Antiillusionismus' and 'eingreifendes Denken' are a matter of people watching plays, not just reading books.

5. Leben des Galilei *on the Stage: 'Denken aus Sinnlichkeit'*

The interaction between Brecht the playwright and Brecht the practical man of the theatre was complex and open-ended, and invariably fruitful. Hardly any of his plays exist in a definitive form and few productions completely satisfied him (although he did once single out Charles Laughton as his ideal Galilei). Testing and revising were crucial parts of the creative process; and testing meant trying out in the theatre as much as rethinking in response to changes in historical circumstances. Our play's chequered *Entstehungsgeschichte* shows Brecht frequently rewriting scenes, adding or subtracting on the basis of insights gained at rehearsal or with specific kinds of audience in mind. Lyon's *Bertolt Brecht in America* contains much relevant information concerning the Los Angeles and New York productions, as does the 1948 'Modellbuch' *Aufbau einer Rolle. Laughtons Galilei* (*BFA*25, pp.7-69). On the Berlin production Käthe Rülicke (*16*, pp.91-152), Werner Hecht and Erich Engel (*18*, pp.112-26) are indispensable. Yet if Brecht had lived to see even this third version beyond the rehearsal process, one suspects the text would have been different again.

Many features of the American version reputedly derive from the unique way in which the German playwright and an English actor who spoke no German 'translated by acting out the lines on which they were working' (*27*, p.172). No wonder the blocking details and stage directions to the Hollywood *Fassung* are more elaborate than those of the pre-war original. Each successive version, in fact, bears witness to the author's flexibility and shows evidence of modification on technical as well as historical grounds.

Most plays suffer from being merely read, not least *Leben des Galilei*, the effects of which depend very much on theatricality: tableau scenes (the handing over of the telescope, the Shrovetide carnival, the masked ball), telling gestures (Galilei being dried with a towel during his first long speech, his being ominously cut dead by Rector Gaffone on the steps of the Medici Palace, his body-language on his reappearance after the recantation, or his exaggeratedly pedagogic posture for much of Scene 14). Words are often contradicted, or enriched, by dramatic context; for instance, the phrase 'Ebenbild Gottes' used by an old cardinal just before his collapse, or the fact that the hair-splitting disputation between Galilei and the scholars was conducted in the presence of representatives of the working class. Above all, *Leben des Galilei* repeatedly dramatizes the act of scientific discovery.

Sense, in many instances, comes via the senses. Galilei's inveterate 'Denken aus Sinnlichkeit' is also his creator's, and it finds its aesthetic correlative in the sensuousness with which ideas are put over. The result is a sustained dramatic appeal to the senses in a series of episodes where carefully controlled décor, supporting music, costume, body-language and an array of choreographed rhythms combine to make the appreciation of 'Dialektik' a 'Genuß' (*GW*16, p.702).

Leaving aside the obvious fact that language becomes an acoustic phenomenon once plays move from the page to the stage, the main sense appealed to here is the visual. Drawing an analogy between his early work and the silent cinema, John Fuegi once suggested that one of Brecht's main objectives was to make his theatre 'intelligible to an audience sitting on the other side of sound-proof glass'. But in the later works, including *Leben des Galilei*, more of a balance is struck between sight and sound; now 'both eye and ear are fully engaged at every moment of the production' (*12*, pp.25f.)

The connexion between the play's content and its visual potential was to the fore even in Brecht's early thinking. In his 1937 'Rede über die Widerstandskraft der Vernunft' he toys with certain images soon to become central to the play's depiction of its protagonist. Describing contemporary scientists being often forced to connive with the state, he conjures up a picture of the compliant physicist:

> Der Physiker muß imstande sein, für den Krieg optische
> Apparate zu konstruieren, die eine sehr weite Sicht
> gewähren, zugleich muß er imstande sein, Vorgänge für
> ihn gefährlichster Art in seiner nächsten Nähe, sagen wir
> an seiner Universität, *nicht* zu sehen. Er hat
> Schutzvorrichtungen zu konstruieren gegen die Angriffe
> fremder Nationen, aber er darf nicht darüber nachdenken,
> was zu machen ist gegen die Angriffe auf ihn von seiten
> der eigenen Behörden. (*GW*20, p.254)

This picture, of an inventor whose optical gadgets offer his political
masters military advantages while he is at the same time having to
turn a blind eye to their dangerous behaviour, finds a powerful
objective correlative in the ensuing play's literal and figurative uses
of the *seeing* motif. The 'optische Apparate' have now become more
specifically a telescope (with the mercantile and military attractions
to the Venetian Republic shown in Scene 2); the physicist is now for
much of the play specifically an astronomer, and he has to turn two
blind eyes in both private and social contexts. Yet although Brecht's
'Rede' makes much of the abuse of science in the service of
belligerents, war remains a largely understated, yet important implicit
dimension of *Leben des Galilei*. Despite shifts in emphasis between
essay and play, the central contradiction remains: that of a boffin who
uses his eyes constructively within his own specialized field, but
displays tunnel vision when it comes to the political repercussions of
both his scholarly work and his general behaviour.

   Galilei's aphorism 'Glotzen ist nicht Sehen' (p.11, in the
Brecht-Laughton version 'gawking is not seeing') has implications not
only for Galilei's astronomical discoveries and his social
blinkeredness, but also for those watching. Audiences have to be
induced to register critically what Galilei either fails to notice or
chooses to underplay. Seeing functions as more than just a plot
ingredient; it is one of the play's main forms of aesthetic
'Sinnlichkeit'. One of Brecht's lifelong guiding principles, Hegel's

dictum that 'Die Wahrheit ist konkret', furnishes a reliable way in to the play's material and its method.

One of the most detailed dramatizations of the need for correct perception comes as early as Scene 1, where Galilei attempts to overcome Andrea's resistance to the heliocentric theory. The starting-point is the fact that the boy's eyes appear to be showing him that the sun *does* move across the sky each day:

> ANDREA Aber ich sehe doch, daß die Sonne abends
> woanders hält als morgens. Da kann sie doch nicht
> stillstehn! Nie und nimmer.
> GALILEI Du siehst! Was siehst du? Du siehst gar nichts.
> Du glotzt nur. Glotzen ist nicht sehen. (p.11)

What follows is an object lesson in the value of critical perception, with Andrea being initiated into approaching 'das Natürliche' as if it were 'auffällig'. This episode would scarcely be so protracted or come so early, were it not needed to demonstrate to the audience the difference between an unquestioning acceptance of surface impressions and genuine interpretative perception.

Galilei's first attempt at persuading Andrea to re-examine the 'evidence' of his own eyes, when observing that the sun is in a different place later in the day than where it came up, involves a simple analogy. Although Andrea dismisses it as misleading ('Nehmen Sie nicht lauter solche Beispiele, Herr Galilei. Damit schaffen Sie's immer', p.13), it is in fact an experimental *Modell* skilfully chosen to bring out the fundamental issues at stake. Just as Brecht's play X-rays history, so Galilei offers a penetrating form of lateral thinking about the solar system. The washstand (its very cumbersomeness suggesting that it is unlikely to move) is made to represent the sun, while the young Andrea, sitting on his chair and carried around by Galilei, stands for Man on the Earth, but now no longer motionless and 'eingekapselt' within the old Ptolemaic system. Using these simple props, Galilei is able to show Andrea that one half-revolution of his chair puts the washstand in a different place *without it having moved*. But the boy senses possibly crucial discrepancies between the demonstration and what it is meant to explain. Having tried to pass on the lesson to his mother (like his mentor, Andrea is also an incorrigible teacher), he returns complaining: 'es stimmt nicht. Den Stuhl mit mir haben Sie nur seitwärts um sich selber gedreht und nicht so. *Macht eine Armbewegung vornüber.* Sonst wäre ich nämlich heruntergefallen [...]. Warum haben Sie den Stuhl nicht vorwärts gedreht? Weil dann bewiesen ist, daß ich von der Erde ebenfalls herunterfallen würde, wenn sie sich so drehen würde' (pp.12f.). With an apple and splinter of wood Galilei then offers a more persuasive model, this time winning Andrea over: 'Das ist fein, das wird sie wundern' (p.14).

These two demonstrations are test cases for Galilei's belief in 'die sanfte Gewalt der Vernunft über die Menschen' (p.34). (Ironically, a visual model is employed to make Andrea suspicious of what his eyes seem to show him.) The differences between Galilei's two illustrations – first washstand and chair, then apple with sliver of wood stuck in it – are instructive as to the mental set being encouraged. One of the drawbacks of Galilei's first attempt is the fact that Andrea, sitting on his chair, is still saddled with his customary perspective. In the second, he is obliged to stand outside himself: to look at a splinter of wood stuck in an apple with enough mental agility to interpret it as representing him standing on a planet, even in an upside-down position. Given these divergences between Models One and Two, it is surprising that Brecht chose to remove the second illustration from the American version and thereby to forfeit an important modification of critical thinking, as well as the all-important apple image (running as a motif right through much of *Leben des Galilei*).

Throughout the entire play, seeing is not simply a matter of believing what is in front of one's nose, but of interpretive observation, a decoding of the significance of what is being shown and a grasp of functional relationships between ingredients. For Brecht, 'das komplexe Sehen muß geübt werden' (*BFA*24, p.59), not only in the sense that it is the *sine qua non* of his kind of social criticism, but because the new theatre has the task of educating its audience to become proficient at it.

Of all the sequences in *Leben des Galilei* where what we perceive during performance is vital to an understanding of what is going on, the enrobing ritual in Scene 12 stands out as depending most on non-verbal elements. It depicts the Cardinal Inquisitor's audience with Pope Urban VIII (formerly Cardinal Barberini), preparing the ground for the interrogation and possible torture of Galilei. The episode prefigures Galilei's own later capitulation, in that the Pope now fails to side with progressive thinking and surrenders to the forces arrayed alongside the Cardinal Inquisitor. The American version highlights the parallel by juxtaposing the statement 'Mr Galilei understands about machinery' (*BFA*5, p.169) with a sub-heading 'POPE URBAN VIII [...] YIELDS TO THE CLERICAL MACHINE (*BFA*5, p.168). At one level, we have the Pope listening to the arguments for arraigning Galilei and gradually succumbing to them (despite his initial 'Nein! Nein! Nein!'), though only up to a certain point: 'Das Alleräußerste ist, daß man ihm die Instrumente zeigt' (p.108). However, verbal exchange is only one dimension to this scene. There is another crucial feature: '*Während der Audienz wird er* [der Papst] *angekleidet. Von außen das Geschlurfe vieler Füße*' (p.105). This image of the Pope being progressively enrobed for the imminent conclave on the Galilei problem accompanies the entire discussion until the point where he appears '*In vollem Ornat*' (p.108).

The dressing sequence is an explanatory comment on the new Pope's shabby behaviour, for it shows us a man who at the start of the scene still retained traces of the old Cardinal Barberini gradually become weighed down by his robes of office to the point where he is imprisoned by them. As Speirs points out, 'this dressing scene recalls, by way of contrast, the opening scene of the play where Galileo [...] appears stripped to the waist' (*35*, p.132). Barberini metamorphoses vestment by vestment into an impersonal functionary, the mere symbol of his office, like the Cardinal Inquisitor whom we only know by his title. Again, the stage directions to the American version makes all·this explicit: 'At the beginning of the scene he is plainly Barberini, but as the scene proceeds he gets more and more obscured by grandiose vestments' (*BFA*5, p.167), until eventually: '*The eyes of*

Barberini look helplessly at the Cardinal Inquisitor from under the completely assembled panoply of Pope Urban VIII' (BFA5, p.169).

An accompanying *Geräuschkulisse*, the shuffling feet on the adjoining corridor, supplies an additional gloss to this episode. One might be tempted to assume a contrast between a static Pope, weighed down by the cumulative symbols of his office, and the people on the move outside. After all, only two scenes before, we had witnessed a very vivid image of history as a carnival procession. But at the end of the meeting Pope Urban finally comments on the disturbance outside: 'eine Unverschämtheit. Dieses Getrampel in den Korridoren ist unerträglich. Kommt denn die ganze Welt?' To which the Cardinal Inquisitor replies: 'Nicht die ganze, aber ihr bester Teil' (p.108). (In the earlier US version, where the commotion had already been complained about right at the outset, the rejoinder is: 'Not the whole world, your Holiness. But a gathering of the faithful', *BFA5*, p.169.) Any putative contrast between an inert Pope and the commotion outside now becomes of subsidiary importance. Either the Cardinal Inquisitor has cunningly arranged this charade to impress upon the Holy Father the momentousness of his decision and isolate him from the 'faithful' majority, or this is an unorchestrated indication of just how far out ahead of orthodox church opinion the Pope risks putting himself if he refuses to endorse the Inquisition's plans. The twin images of him imprisoned within his vestments and being virtually blackmailed into submission by the intimidating noise on the corridor goes some way towards presenting the Pope's behaviour in terms of cause and effect, even if contextual pressures can no more exonerate him than they will Galilei.

The 'Fastnacht' carnival also gains much from staging. Here, 'das Volk' reveals that it has realized the revolutionary potential contained in Galilei's teachings. Scene 10 thus foreshadows Vanni's confident claim 'Hinter Ihnen stehen die oberitalienischen Städte, Herr Galilei' (p.101). Located in the market place of an unspecified Italian town on Shrove Tuesday 1632 (the year in which Galilei's explosive *Dialogue* appeared in Florence), this sequence makes clear that certain elements of Italian society have really comprehended the wider social significance of the new discoveries, even if the

Establishment fails to understand, or chooses to suppress, such uncomfortable truths.

Although the cavalcade is mounted by the trade guilds, there are at least three distinct classes on stage during this scene: the *Lumpenproletariat* (the singer and his family), the artisan class (who perform the main pageant) and, as the 1957 Berlin production emphasized through its use of sumptuous costumes, the rich merchant class among the onlookers. For the moment, these classes still co-exist peacefully; but this will not last much longer.

In the original version of *Leben des Galilei*, Brecht appended the following comment to the episode:

> *Diese Szene kann in eine Ballettszene aufgelöst werden.*
> *Im Stil von Brueghels STREIT DES KARNIVALS MIT DEN*
> *FASTEN kann ein Volksfastnachtstreiben gezeigt werden.*
> *Nach der ersten Strophe der Moritat kann sich ein*
> *Fastnachtszug auf den Platz bewegen, in dem eine BIBEL*
> *schreitet, die ein Loch bekommen hat, ein Wagen mit*
> *einem Globus gezogen wird, auf dem ein Mönch*
> *ausgestreckt mit beiden Armen einen abrutschenden*
> *STUHL PETRI zu halten sucht usw. Dann, vor der letzten*
> *Strophe, können der MOND, die SONNE, die ERDE und*
> *die Planeten auftreten, die das alte und neue*
> *Bewegungssystem im Tanz, zu einer strengen Musik,*
> *vorführen. (BFA5, p.82)*

The two later versions opt for a clearer division between the ballad part of the scene and the procession itself, using a different way of presenting the importance of Galilei's discoveries. The Brueghelesque visual quality is retained in the costumes and casting, but the ballet element is transferred from the carnival procession to the actions of the singer and his family, who, before the appearance of the procession proper, entertain the waiting crowd with a *Moritat*, a form of popular folk-ballad associated with both fairground and market place. The song, 'das neueste Florentiner Lied, das man in ganz Oberitalien singt' (p.94), comes from the seat of feudal power within the state, but also from the very city which has just seen the publication of Galilei's new challenge to the Establishment's authority. The performance echoes earlier moments in the play. The man's patter to the effect that this is a song 'das wir mit großen Kosten hier importiert haben' is reminiscent of earlier exorbitant claims about how much time and labour it had cost Galilei to invent the telescope presented to the Republic of Venice (both he and the ballad-singers have been forced into trickery by economic pressures).

The stage directions for the mime which wife and child perform to the singer's ballad read:

> [...] *Das Weib und das Kind treten vor. Das Weib hält ein rohes Abbild der Sonne, und das Kind, über dem Kopf einen Kürbis, Abbild der Erde, haltend, umkreist das Weib. Der Sänger deutet exaltiert auf das Kind, als vollführe es einen gefährlichen Salto mortale, wenn es auf einzelne Trommelschläge ruckartig Schritt für Schritt macht.* [...]. (p.97)

Two things here are of significance: first, the shabbiness of the props: the 'rohes Abbild der Sonne' and the pumpkin (the American version even had the child merely carrying 'a cardboard pumpkin' (*BFA*5, p.163), as if its family were too poor to be able to afford the real vegetable that they need as a prop); second, the contrived precariousness of the child's movements, as if to communicate the fact that people are as yet unused to their new-found freedoms, even when they merely savour them with the fool's licence that carnival affords. The idea of the dangerous somersault serves to stress that what the family are presenting comes (and has to do so) in the protective guise of a ballad with a strict cautionary didactic purpose. On the surface, it looks as if it is warning against any such dangerous new-fangled ideas; in fact, many of the song's stanzas daringly spell out the revolutionary implication of the new astronomy, only to retreat thereafter to a pose of cautious inertia. Since the ballad is taken over (in German translation) almost verbatim from the California version where the stage directions of the Brecht/Laughton version are far more explicit than those in the play's final form, it is worth looking at how *Galileo* indicated the way certain features of the song should be performed.

Toying with the possibility of her emancipation as a woman (i.e. someone lower than her husband in the scale of creation), the singer's wife, hitherto condemned to contribute no more than a subservient drum accompaniment to the male's performance, finally resists. We are told in the American version, she '*gives baby to Child and comes forward*' to sing the line: 'Now that I come to think of it, I feel / That I could also use a change'. The husband's response ('No, no, no, no, no, no, stop, Galileo, stop!', *BFA5*, pp.162f.) ostensibly expresses his fear that social chaos will prevail if such new-fangled thoughts are allowed to proliferate, yet at the same time we get the impression that everyone would like to be his or her own master, even if this is dismissed as no more than a pipe dream.

The stage directions which follow have the family emphasizing the shockingness of the ballad's predictions by stopping drumming and dancing whenever a particularly alarming possibility is lighted upon in the song:

> Why each of us would say and do just as he pleases,
> > as he pleases,
> > as he pleases,
> *His Wife stops drumming. Child stands still.* (*BFA5*, p.161)

The sudden, estranging, cessation of noise gives a pause for the disturbing nature of what is being described to sink in. Yet at the same time it suggests that it is as disturbing to the singer and his family as it would be, according to the Little Monk, to his ageing parents in the Campagna (p.76). Yet for all that, it is also possible to detect a goodly measure of irony in the performance. If it is only in the form of a condemnation that the family can predict the repercussions of Galilei's findings, then so be it; one could find enough historical equivalents to their Schweykian behaviour at the time. But by presenting their material in this way, the performers at the same time send up the kneejerk Establishment reaction to

Galilei's 'erschröckliche Lehre' (through exaggerated movements and mime).

When the carnival procession comes on the scene, there is more forthrightness to the floats' depiction of what Galilei's teaching means for society. The gloves are now off. A figure representing the Grand Duke of Florence is displayed looking through a telescope; or as the caption puts it, 'Schaut aus nach Verdruß' (either he looks as if he is in an unenviable predicament or is literally looking through his telescope for trouble). A doll dressed in cardinal's vestments is menacingly tossed in the air, whilst a dwarf (an image applied to the lackey scientist in Scene 14) contextualizes the whole event with the placard 'Das neue Zeitalter'. The cavalcade's *pièce de résistance* comes in the form of 'eine überlebensgroße Puppe, Galileo Galilei', preceded by a child carrying a gigantic Bible the pages of which have been crossed out. For predictable reasons, it is the singer, not the guild members, who is given the honour of supplying a caption to this image: 'Galileo Galileo, der Bibelzertrümmerer!' Evidently, both the singer and the guilds organizing the carnival procession are able to look further down the road of history than Galilei still dares to, but they have distinct class interests for doing so. As we are often reminded, such people have much to gain from a more favourable response to Galilei's findings. Perhaps this explains the poverty of the procession. While the earlier introduction of the itinerant singer and his family as 'ein halb verhungertes Schauspielpaar' (p.94) rings true – they are, after all, little more than penniless buskers or performing beggars – the guild procession, with its 'Männer in Lumpen', may seem more surprising. Like Mardi Gras, these festivities were usually marked by lavish displays. Brecht, however, wished to exaggerate the contrast between the kind of rich pageant that the aristocracy (the Venetian Republic in Scene 2, Roman high society in Scene 7) were capable of mounting, and the destitution of those further down the social ladder who appreciate what Galilei's findings can mean for them and their children's children.

Brecht approved of Walter Benjamin's remark that the real hero of *Leben des Galilei* was 'das Volk' (*18*, p.56). Yet with the notable exceptions of Frau Sarti, Andrea, Federzoni and the little

Monk, the common people are more conspicuous by their absence, except in the carnival scene. Here, both their poverty and clearsightedness are highlighted. The exceptional occasion gives them licence to act out the future implications of Galilei's astronomy, albeit in the form of a caveat: 'Geehrte Einwohner, solche Lehren sind ganz unmöglich', not to be tolerated, that is, because they threaten 'die Große Ordnung, ordo ordinum', the 'regula aeternis' (p.95). Nevertheless the occasion which grants them this liberty is a church festival ('All Fools' Day' in the American version, Shrove Tuesday in the final one). Their emancipation is short-lived, but it is staged in such a way as to stir in the audience images of later revolutions and times when it will no longer be contained within the time repressively allotted it by the Christian calendar.

Scene 10's 'Vorgeschmack der Zukunft' is strategically positioned immediately after the scene in which Galilei responds to the installation of the new pope by returning to astronomy. In its vibrancy and historical enthusiasm the carnival episode also contrasts sharply with the following gloomy scene, where the heretical astronomer is summoned to Rome by the Inquisition and where he fails to respond to Vanni's overtures. Although it may appear to be little more than an interlude when read in print, Scene 10, one of the theatrical highlights of the play, will take considerably more performance time than reading it might suggest. Of course, not all scenes may be as dependent for their effect on stage realization as this one is, but in virtually every episode staging details make an important contribution.

Throughout, great emphasis is placed on the *Bühnenbild* against which words, gestures and actions are to be experienced by the audience. Indeed, one could conclude that it is décor that makes a play by Brecht immediately recognizable as Brechtian. 'An Stätten, wo gearbeitet wird, liest man oft: "Unbeschäftigten ist der Zutritt untersagt". Das sollten die Bühnenbauer über ihr Spielfeld hängen', Brecht wrote. What he meant by this is summed up in the title of the essay, 'Das Nötigste ist genug' (*GW*15, p.453), in other words, all aspects of the stage set must have a function to perform, otherwise they are redundant. Staging will to some considerable extent involve principles of abstraction and reduction. As Brecht pointed out in 'Über die Kargheit', 'Die Beschränkung auf das Notwendige (Mitspielende) macht den Bühnenbau mitunter karg aussehend. [...] Karg wirkt auch, daß der nichtillusionistische Bühnenbau sich mit Andeutungen der Merkmale begnügt, mit Abstraktionen arbeitet' (*GW*15, pp.452f.) In contrast to the clutter of Naturalist detail against which Brecht often polemicized, stage props are kept to a minimum, with sets becoming stylized, even to the point of using little more than black cloths surmounted by the scene title to form a clinical backdrop. Obviously, such paring to the essential combats any impression of historical drama set in a faithfully reconstructed three-dimensional period reality. Décor thus becomes an important agent of *Antiillusionismus*. A radically pruned set combined with bold illumination also helps create a consciously *sachlich* atmosphere where attention is focused on characters and how they behave, with little to distract from analytical perception ('die gewünschte Konzentration', as it is called in the discussion of another form of artifice: 'Die Sichtbarkeit der Lichtquellen', *GW*15, p.454).

Brecht's attitude to staging is, as Barthes (*5*, p.87) and Wekwerth (*39*, pp.320ff.) were quick to appreciate, largely semiotic. His essay 'Zeichen und Symbole' (*GW*15, pp.455-58), with its contrast between traditional realistic props and his own use of 'Embleme' and mere 'Kennzeichen für die Schauplätze', gives useful pointers in this direction. But his signs are not always artificial: he often favours the use on stage of what he proudly calls 'ganz dicke, realistische Dinge' (*GW*15, p.457). Thus, the play's seventeenth-century astronomical instruments are accurate reproductions, although even such a pragmatic device can signal added meaning when Galilei encases it in red leather (the token colour of socialism). The astrolabe in Scene 1, a prop which Brecht researched for accuracy, nevertheless becomes an image of 'Einkapselung'; hence the later breaking of the Ptolemaic model in the quarrel in Scene 4 (p.43) is an omen. Even something as representational as period clothing acquires sign function. 'Although the costumes for the American production were *based* on historically verifiable fashions', according to Speirs, 'features which signalled social difference were

exaggerated to make these differences clearer to a modern audience'
(*35*, p.135). Exaggerated costume, be it that of the Venetian Doge's
sumptuous retinue in Scene 2 or of the Vatican dignitaries at a
number of junctures, could make very palpable the connexion
between wealth and power. Other significant contrasts – above all,
between pomp and modesty, inertia and energy – are also
communicated by costume contrasts.

In *Aufbau einer Rolle*, Brecht talks about the patterning of
costume-colours ('das Farbenschema') in *Leben des Galilei*:

> Jede Szene mußte einen Grundton haben – die erste z.B.
> einen zarten matinalen mit Weiß, Gelb und Grau. Aber
> die Gesamtheit der Szenen mußte dann ihre Entwicklung
> haben in der Farbe. In der ersten Szene kam etwa ein
> distinguiertes Tiefblau hinein durch den Ludovico
> Marsili, und dieses Tiefblau blieb auch, abgesondert, in
> der zweiten Szene mit den Großbürgern in ihren
> schwärzlichgrünen, aus Filz und Leder gemachten
> Röcken. Der gesellschaftliche Aufstieg des Galilei wurde
> auch in den Farben sichtbar. Das Silber und Perlgrau der
> vierten (Hof-) Szene leitete über in ein Notturno in Braun
> und Schwarz (Verspottung des Galilei durch die Mönche
> des Collegium Romanum) zu der achten, dem Ball der
> Kardinäle   mit   den   phantastischen   delikaten
> Einzelmasken (Damen und Herren) zwischen den
> Kardinälen in Karmesin. Dies war ein Ausbruch der
> Farbe, aber ihre Entfesselung kam noch, und zwar in der
> neunten, der Fastnachts-Szene. Wie die Kardinäle und
> der Adel hatte auch das niedere Volk sein Maskenfest.
> Danach kommt der Abstieg in die stumpfen und grauen
> Farben. (*16*, p.46)

Costumes are variously choreographed to produce whole patterns of
significance, the most obvious being the traditional one of *Sein*
contrasting with the *Schein* of a feudal authority soon to wane. Fuegi
(*12*, p.97) explores in some detail the costume patterning in the play,

the alternations between bright and dark colours, reflecting the fluctuations between public and private scenes, as well as moods of optimism and pessimism.

Characters' attire occurs in meaningful configurations, but other stage props also form part of complexes of signals to the audience. Galilei's first words at the start of the play, 'Stell die Milch auf den Tisch, aber klapp kein Buch zu' (p.7), concentrate our attention on two objects which are to become emblems of the twin ingredients of the protagonist's make-up: his sensual and his intellectual appetites. Often the effect is to imbue the few objects placed on stage with a great deal of meaning. They become *objets parlants*, and their significance is often played upon cumulatively.

Milk and books are the same two things Galilei demands during the plague scene (pp.56f.), so his selfishness is again emphasized, as well as his dedication to science. At the end of the play Andrea will smuggle a 'book' (the *Discorsi*) across the border, while pausing to leave a jug of milk for the old woman (p.131). The widening from the specific image of milk to Galilei's other physical and intellectual pleasures (wine, geese, the sheer pleasure of washing, methodically experimenting and even pontificating) usually means that images first introduced as visual impressions, stage props even, gradually tend to evolve to find their place in a whole chain of related images and metaphors. Thus, when Andrea is asked by Galilei to describe the astrolabe at the beginning of the first scene, he says at one point: 'in der Mitte ist ein kleiner Stein' (p.8). The image will be taken up later when Galilei lets his *Beweisstein* fall every so often (the operative contrast being between the small stone imprisoned at the centre of the astrolabe and the moving stone subject to the force of gravity and suggesting the new rotating Earth). But falling, as we saw in the chapter on alienation, is suggestive in another sense, for it refers to Galilei's 'Fall' in the biblical sense (an idea which is most explicitly emphasized at the end of the recantation scene). Similarly, the debate between Galilei and Andrea in Scene 1 is reprised in Scene 13 when Galilei's followers read the time off a sundial, an object which misleadingly appears to depend on measuring the *movement* of the sun.

If Brechtian staging has as one of its functions a highlighting of the content's dialectical implications, then one of its strategies is to make the audience aware of contradictions between various scenes and even within them. Galilei, for instance, complains in Scene 2 about having to go through the demeaning 'Karnival' of handing over the telescope to the Venetian authorities (p.24), but it will to some considerable extent be the task of the staging to give substance to this word by highlighting the differences between this carnivalesque scene and at least two others in the play: the Shrovetide pageant and the masked ball, with its threats, deceptions and veneer of courtesy. Staging will also bear a good measure of the burden of bringing out parallels between the plague scene, where Galilei continues working, despite the threat, and the recantation scene where he succumbs. The plague episode does not simply confront the audience with the idea of a natural disaster. With the image of the *cordon sanitaire* thrown around Galilei's street and the soldiers forcing him back into his house ('*Mit ihren langen Spießen schieben sie Galilei in sein Haus zurück. Hinter ihm verrammeln sie das Tor*', p.54), it shows the way in which nature even gives society a further excuse to exercize repression.

Another feature common to the two scenes, and one which comes over powerfully on stage, is the superstition/religion analogy. In both cases, the emphasis is acoustic. During the plague scene our attention is drawn to a *Geräuschkulisse*: '*Ein klapperndes Geräusch wird hörbar*' (p.55). Inquiring about it, Galilei is told: 'Sie versuchen, mit Geräuschen die Wolken zu vertreiben, in denen die Pestkeime sind'. Galilei's laughter at this remnant from the Dark Ages for a moment drowns out the ominous sound of irrational thinking at work. However, the real operative contrast is not between two noises (rattle and laughter), but between what they betoken: late-feudal superstition and modern science (which will be able to tackle the plague in more meaningful ways). Another acoustic effect, the bell of St Mark's which rings out in Scene 13 to announce that Galilei has recanted and which is welcomed by Virginia as a sign of redemption ('Er ist nicht verdammt!' p.112), is in fact more like the death-knell of progress. Hence, at two key moments sounds off stage, associated with superstition or the irrational, give a sense of encircling threat to the characters we see before us.

Both scenes are modifications of a technique of staging which Brecht makes great use of: that of dividing attention, frequently through the use of the split stage. In a pioneering study of this aspect of Brecht's technique, Andrzej Wirth applied the term 'Stereometrie' to such splitting (*41*, p.346). Usually, the bipartite stage is employed for aesthetic distancing. In Scene 4, we are aware of the tussle going on between Andrea and Grand Duke Cosmo 'oben im Arbeitszimmer', while Galilei and the visiting dignitaries enter his 'Studierzimmer'. In this case, further contrasts are spatialized by the split-level layout: between children and grown-ups, between those interested in what the telescope has to show and those seeking little more than a disputation; between those able to speak to each other as equals and those who know their social places. Such spatialization, a form of dramatic irony in that we see more than either party on stage can, facilitates greater insight into what is happening. Indeed, the contrast in Scenes 4 and 13 between what we can see before us and what we imagine to be happening elsewhere is an extension of this principle. Elsewhere, we have contrasts between what Virginia and Frau Sarti are preoccupied with at the same time as important scientific experiments are being conducted in another part of the room; between the mocking behaviour of the priests outside the Collegium Romanum and Galilei comporting himself with dignity, anxious to hear Clavius's verdict; between the events at the masked ball and, in the wings, the Cardinal Inquisitor's ominous encounter with Virginia. All of these juxtapositions generate forms of 'komplexes Sehen', because two groups of happenings are being presented simultaneously and one cannot identify with two sets of characters at once. What Brecht in another context calls 'Vergleichendes Blättern', the audience's ability to gain particular insights from the mental juxtaposition of two separate parts of the play, here becomes a spatial presentation of contradictory elements. Whereas the page can only present such elements in the form of a *Nacheinander*, on the stage the principle of *Nebeneinander* tends to be much more to the fore.

When it came to the astronomical wranglings that had to be made comprehensible to a modern audience, Brecht entertained various staging possibilities: 'in der vierten Szene kann man die Phasen der Venus zeigen', in Scene 7 'können auf dem Schirm [...] die Sonnenflecken wandernd gezeigt werden' (*BFA*24, p.234), although at a later stage he was to have practical misgivings about the use of projections: 'Keine Projektionen, da die Bühne dann nicht voll beleuchtet werden kann. Eventuell riesige Fotos' (*BFA*23, p.251). One of the points which Brecht makes here in 'Zur Regie' implies a less obvious function for certain projected images than one has, say, with the montage of Galilei's embarrassingly sycophantic letter to the Grand Duke of Florence at the conclusion to Scene 3 (p.39) or of the *Discorsi* extract at the end of the recantation scene (p.114). For both in the case of the phases-of-Venus and the sunspot episodes Brecht regards the accompanying astronomical images as much more than a purely subordinate background illustration of the discoveries being made on stage at the time. Of the 'Phasen der Venus' projection he says: 'Man kann dazu Galilei hören'; and of the sunspots discovery: 'Auch hier kann, am besten durch Andrea, beschrieben werden, was gesehen wird'. The words, in effect, are no more than a commentary to the concretely visual.

This is also one of the many instances in the play of what Brecht called 'Literarisierung' (*GW*15, pp.464f.): a situation (as in the case of the Shrovetide carnival episode) where actions, events, even characters and gestures, are verbalized. Sometimes in advance ('Stell die Milch auf den Tisch, aber klapp kein Buch zu'), sometimes simultaneously (as with the astronomical examples in Scene 1), and occasionally in retrospect (e.g. the two projected scene-ending quotations mentioned above). 'Literarisierung' is a form of duplication. What we can in any case observe is also rendered in language: 'DER THEOLOGE *das zerbrochene Ptolemäische Modell am Boden sehend*: Hier scheint etwas entzweigegangen' (p.44); or of the meaningful change in colour of the telescope casing: 'LUDOVICO [...] Ich sah, Sie machten das Futteral rot. In Holland war es grün' (p.25); or 'DER ERSTE GELEHRTE *zu Galilei*: Herr Galilei, Ihnen ist etwas hinabgefallen' (p.61); or '*In diesem Augenblick beginnt die*

Glocke von Sankt Markus zu dröhnen [...] VIRGINIA [...] Die Glocke von Sankt Markus!' (p.112). Brecht's play is peppered with such devices which might at first seem like unnecessary duplications of the obvious. Indeed, in his discussion of the most well-known example of 'Literarisierung', 'Über Titel' (*GW*15, pp.465ff.), Brecht confronts the objection that the titles he uses at the beginning of scenes (and, in the case of *Leben des Galilei*, also the little songs) might be considered 'überflüssig'. His arguments here, coupled with his practice, show quite clearly that verbal commentaries of this kind, while they may duplicate information, are far from superfluous because they serve a number of further functions.

With two exceptions (Scenes 5 and 10), the individual scenes of *Leben des Galilei* come equipped with both projected or suspended titles (giving information about what is to happen in them) and 'Vorstrophen': short songs giving the nitty-gritty of a particular scene in an epigrammatic form, e.g.

Die Wahrheit im Sacke
Die Zung in der Backe
Schwieg er acht Jahre, dann war's ihm zu lang.
Wahrheit, geh deinen Gang. (p.80)

These 'Vorstrophen', even the two words 'DER PAPST' at the start of Scene 12, were set to music by Hanns Eisler (cf. the extracts from this music published in *3*) and were intended for performance by three singers, decked out as choirboys and thus parodistically presenting the socialist commentary to the play as if it were a litany. The instrumental accompaniment was supplied by flute, clarinet and harpsichord, augmented, where appropriate, by piccolo and, of course, the singer's wife's drum. The choirboys were an alto, a soprano and a mezzo-soprano. Eisler already furnished the music for most of these 'Vorstrophen' (together with the Medici madrigal in Scene 7, pp.65, 69) for the Los Angeles premiere. He also set the carnival scene to music, an important detail since it establishes a significant stylistic bridge between the musical commentary to the individual scenes and the 'Vorgeschmack der Zukunft' which might be thought of as offering a historicizing commentary to the entire play. According to Lucchesi and Shull (*27*, item 261), it is unlikely that Eisler's music was used for the German premiere (there seems to have been some problem with accommodating the German words to Eisler's score); moreover, even for the Berlin version Brecht could not obtain the singers he wanted and had to use tape-recordings.

On the whole, this use of sung words as an elevated commentary to the action of a work gives much more prominence to the commentary element in performance than it achieves on the page. In the printed version of the carnival scene, for instance, Brecht has to make do with indentation to mark a contrast between the sung and spoken words of the ballad-singer, a contrast which obviously becomes more pronounced in performance. The mini-songs illustrate the fact that 'Literarisierung' can entail words augmented by acoustic or visual elements. The placards bearing the titles to the individual scenes are presented visually, and one reacts very differently to a scene which has its heading displayed above it for its entire duration than to a scene which is simply read on the page and whose title comes and goes as one turns the page.

The kind of 'Literarisierung' of stage effects we have been looking at serves a variety of purposes, the first being to remind us of what kind of theatre we are watching. If life is 'titellos' (*GW*15, p.464), then the main aim of such titles ('1633: DIE INQUISITION BEORDERT DEN WELTBEKANNTEN FORSCHER NACH ROM', '1637: GALILEIS BUCH "DISCORSI" ÜBERSCHREITET DIE ITALIENISCHE GRENZE' etc.) is to function as a token of 'anti-illusionistisches Theater'. Some titles may also be inserted, Brecht claimed, 'damit der Zuschauer vom "Was" zum "Wie" übergehen kann' (*GW*15, p.464). That is to say, if the titles inform us in advance what is going to happen in a scene, then attention will be focused much more on the mechanics of how this comes about. In actual fact, scene-headings seldom signal *all* the main things that are going to happen in the ensuing scene. Usually, the technique entails a cat-and-mouse game with the audience, telegraphing some of the events that follow, but by no means always the most important ones. To be told that the carnival scene takes place in 1632 does little to enlighten us as to the significance of that date; and to entitle another scene 'DER

PAPST' hardly gives much away. Brecht's practice in this respect is much less mechanical and more varied than his theory would suggest.

When discussing 'Literarisierung' Brecht generally widens the subject beyond simple verbalization to cover a situation where a whole variety of 'Sprüche, Photographien und Sinnbilder stehen um die agierenden Personen' (*GW*15, p.464). The term seems to suggest glossing devices of various orders, techniques whose commenting function will be enhanced by the artificiality with which they are staged.

A few of the staging devices demanded by the author for *Leben des Galilei* may seem simplistic, possibly even 'cheap' to a modern sophisticated public. To have the geriatric cardinal collapse in Scene 6 immediately after his panegyric to Man as created in God's image and therefore 'unvergänglich' (p.62) may strike some as too clumsy by far (on a par with the double entendre which follows: 'Eure Eminenz haben sich zuviel zugemutet!', or the adolescent punning on 'Schwindel' at the start of the episode). Similarly, to have Cardinals Bellarmin and Barberini wearing, of all things, the masks of lamb and dove in Scene 7 comes over as too laboured, especially when the point has to be reinforced by the nudging remark 'nehmen wir wieder unsere Masken vor. Der arme Galilei hat keine' (p.70).

To be sure, some of these seemingly crude effects exploit the obvious for humorous or estranging reasons, but this can hardly give Brecht carte blanche for his entire repertoire of deliberately transparent effects, any more than it lets us condone all of his more juvenile puns. Nevertheless, it is worth bearing in mind that effects which come over as banal or patronizing in the cold light of print can be redeemed by an immediacy of effect, when seen on the stage. As Brecht never tired of repeating, 'the proof of the pudding is in the eating'.

It has been suggested that 'almost the entire burden of preventing audience identification with Galileo was to come not from the text but from the production' (*12*, p.92). But in the earlier exploration of *Verfremdung*, we saw that a substantial amount of distancing is nevertheless linguistic. In any case, it would be wrong to interpret all the visual effects and forms of dramatic 'Sinnlichkeit' demanded by a production of *Leben des Galilei* as no more than an extension of his arsenal of *Verfremdungseffekte*. In reality, they relate to various further factors: the mistrust of language as an expression of false consciousness, a desire to reveal the materialist nature of truth, a keen sense of what is pedagogically most effective and a sheer joy in the potential of the theatre.

Although Brecht later spoke dismissively of his failure to be radical enough in exploiting this theatrical dimension in the case of *Leben des Galilei* ('technisch ein großer rückschritt [...] man müßte das stück vollständig neu schreiben [...] alles auf planetarische demonstrationen gestellt', *1*, p.32), one should not underestimate the powerful potential of the play's stage effects. The text, in the words of the old adage, is merely a pretext; and what it is a pretext for is stunningly good theatre.

Select Bibliography

A. BERTOLT BRECHT'S WRITINGS

1. *Arbeitsjournal*, 3 vols, ed. Werner Hecht (Frankfurt a. M., Suhrkamp, 1973).
2. *Briefe*, ed. Günter Glaeser, 2 vols (Frankfurt a. M., Suhrkamp, 1981).
3. 'Verse zu *Leben des Galilei*', *Versuche 15: 'Die Tage der Commune', 'Die Dialektik auf dem Theater', 'Zu "Leben des Galilei"', Drei Reden, Zwei Briefe* (Berlin, Suhrkamp, 1957), pp.110-33.

B. CRITICAL LITERATURE ON BRECHT

4. Arendt, Hannah, 'Der Dichter Bertolt Brecht', *Die Neue Rundschau*, 61 (1950), 53-67.
5. Barthes, Roland, *Essais critiques* (Paris, Editions du Seuil, 1964).
6. Borchardt, Frank K., 'Marx, Engels and Brecht's Galilei', *Brecht heute*, 2 (1972), 149-63.
7. Déghaye, Pierre, *Galilée marxiste et le mysticisme astral. Essai sur 'La Vie de Galilée' par Bertolt Brecht* (Paris, éditions de la différence, 1977).
8. Dickson, Keith A., *Towards Utopia. A Study of Brecht* (Oxford, Clarendon Press, 1978).
9. Dieckmann, Friedrich, '*Galilei*-Komplikationen', *Weimarer Beiträge*, 34,2 (1988), 213-29.
10. Esslin, Martin, *Brecht. A Choice of Evils* (London, Eyre and Spottiswoode, 1959).
11. Fehn, Ann Clark, 'Vision and blindness in Brecht's *Leben des Galilei*', *The Germanic Review*, 53 (1978), 27-34.
12. Fuegi, John, *Bertolt Brecht. Chaos, According to Plan* (Cambridge University Press, 1987).
13. —, *The Life and Lies of Bertolt Brecht* (London, Harper Collins, 1994).
14. Grimm, Roderick, *Verfremdung in Bertolt Brechts 'Leben des Galilei'* (Frankfurt a. M., Lang, 1987).
15. Groseclose, John Sidney, 'Sc. 12 of Brecht's *Galilei*. A Structural Study', *Monatshefte*, 62 (1970), 367-82.

16. Hecht, Werner, ed., *Materialien zu Brechts 'Leben des Galilei'* (Frankfurt a. M., Suhrkamp, 1963).

17. —, ed., *Materialien zu Brechts 'Der kaukasische Kreidekreis'* (Frankfurt a. M., Suhrkamp, 1966).

18. —, ed., *Brechts 'Leben des Galilei'* (Frankfurt a. M., Suhrkamp, 1981).

19. Hiley, Jim, *Theatre at Work. The Story of the National Theatre's Production of Brecht's 'Galileo'* (London, Routledge & Kegan Paul, 1981).

20. Jendreiek, Helmut, *Bertolt Brecht. Drama der Veränderung* (Düsseldorf, Bagel, 1969).

21. Knopf, Jan, 'Brecht und die Naturwissenschaften', *Brecht Jahrbuch* (1978), 13-38.

22. —, *Brecht Handbuch: Theater. Eine Ästhetik der Widersprüche* (Stuttgart, Metzler, 1980).

23. Knust, Herbert, 'Brechts Dialektik vom Fressen und von der Moral', *Brecht heute*, 3 (1973), 221-50.

24. —, *Bertolt Brecht. 'Leben des Galilei'* (Frankfurt a. M., Diesterweg, 1992).

25. Ley, Ralph J., 'Francis Bacon, *Galileo* and the Brechtian Theater', in *Essays on Brecht. Theater and Politics*, ed. Siegfried Mews and Herbert Knust (Chapel Hill, University of North Carolina Press, 1974), pp.174-89.

26. Livingstone, R. S., 'Is Galilei a Tui?', in *Antipodische Aufklärungen: Festschrift für Leslie Bodi*, ed. Walter Veit (Frankfurt a. M., Lang, 1987), pp.241-58.

27. Lucchesi, Joachim, and Ronald K. Shull, *Musik bei Brecht* (Frankfurt a. M., Suhrkamp, 1988).

28. Lyon, James K., *Bertolt Brecht in America* (Princeton University Press, 1980).

29. Lyons, Charles R., 'The Life of Galileo. The Focus of Ambiguity in the Villain Hero', *The Germanic Review*, 41 (1966), 57-71.

30. Morley, Michael, *Brecht. A Study* (London, Heinemann, 1977).

31. Müller, Klaus-Detlef, *Die Funktion der Geschichte im Werk Bertolt Brechts. Studien zum Verhältnis von Marxismus und Ästhetik* (Tübingen, Niemeyer, 1967).

32. Nägele, Rainer, 'Zur Struktur von Brechts *Leben des Galilei*', *Der Deutschunterricht*, 23 (1971), 86-99.

33. Sautermeister, Gert, 'Zweifelskunst, abgebrochene Dialektik, blinde Stellen: *Leben des Galilei* (3. Fassung, 1955)', in Walter Hinderer, ed., · *Brechts Dramen. Neue Interpretationen* (Stuttgart, Reclam, 1984), pp.125-61.

34. Schumacher, Ernst, *Drama und Geschichte. Bertolt Brechts 'Leben des Galilei' und andere Stücke* (Berlin, Henschel, 1965).

35. Speirs, Ronald, *Bertolt Brecht* (London, Macmillan, 1987).

36. Szczesny, Gerhard, *Bertolt Brechts 'Leben des Galilei' : Dichtung und Wirklichkeit* (Bonn, Bouvier, 1986).
37. Thomson, Peter, and Glendyr Sacks, *The Cambridge Companion to Brecht* (Cambridge University Press, 1994).
38. Weber, Betty Nance, '*The Life of Galileo* and the Theory of Revolution in Permanence', in *Bertolt Brecht. Political Theory and Literary Practice*, ed. Betty Nance Weber and Hubert Heinen (Manchester University Press, 1980), pp.60-78.
39. Wekwerth, Manfred, *Schriften: Arbeit mit Brecht* (Berlin, Henschel, 1973).
40. White, Alfred D., '*The Life of Galileo*', *Bertolt Brecht's Great Plays* (London, Macmillan, 1978), pp.53-84.
41. Wirth, Andrzej, 'Über die stereometrische Struktur der Brechtschen Stücke', *Sinn und Form: Zweites Sonderheft Bertolt Brecht*, 9 (1957), 346-87.
42. Wyss, Monika, ed., *Brecht in der Kritik. Rezensionen aller Brecht-Aufführungen sowie ausgewählter deutsch- und fremdsprachiger Premieren. Eine Dokumentation* (Munich, Kindler, 1977).
43. Zimmermann, Werner, *Bertolt Brecht: 'Leben des Galilei'. Dramatik der Widersprüche* (Paderborn, Schöningh, 1985).

C. OTHER SOURCES

44. Carver, Terrell, ed., *The Cambridge Companion to Marx* (Cambridge University Press, 1991).
45. Dähnhardt, Willy and Birgit S. Nielsen, eds., *Exil in Dänemark. Deutschsprachige Wissenschaftler, Künstler und Schriftsteller im dänischen Exil nach 1933* (Heide, Westholsteinische Verlagsanstalt Boyens, 1993).
46. Deutscher, Isaac, *The Prophet Outcast. Trotsky: 1929-1940* (London, Oxford University Press, 1963).
47. Döblin, Alfred, 'Bemerkungen zum Roman', *Die Neue Rundschau* (March, 1917), 410-13.
48. Elster, John, *An Introduction to Karl Marx* (Cambridge University Press, 1986).
49. Klaus, Georg, and Manfred Buhr, *Marxistisch-Leninistisches Wörterbuch der Philosophie*, 3 vols (Reinbek, Rowohlt, 1972).
50. Klotz, Volker, *Geschlossene und offene Form im Drama* (Munich, Kohlhammer, 1962).
51. Lenin, Vladimir Ilyich, 'On Dialectics', *Selected Works*, ed. J. Fineberg, Vol. 11: *The Theoretical Principles of Marxism* (London, Lawrence and Wishart, 1943), pp.65-81.

52. Mao Tse-Tung, 'On Contradiction', in *Four Essays on Philosophy*
     (Peking, Foreign Languages Press, 1968), pp.23-78.
53. Marx, Karl, *Kritik der politischen Ökonomie*, in Karl Marx and
     Friedrich Engels, *Werke*, Vol. 13, ed. Institut für Marxismus und
     Leninismus (Berlin, 1964).
54. Mudry, Anna, 'Annäherung an Galileo Galilei', in Anna Mudry (ed.):
     Galileo Galilei: Schriften, Briefe, Dokumente, 2 vols (Munich, Beck,
     1987), pp.7-41.
55. Redondi, Pietro, *Galileo Heretic*, tr. Raymond Rosenthal
     (Harmondsworth, Allen Lane, 1988).
56. Reed, T. J., *Genesis: Some Episodes in Literary Creation. The 1994
     Bithell Memorial Lecture* (London, Institute of Germanic Studies,
     1995).
57. Ronan, Colin A., *Galileo* (London, Weidenfeld and Nicolson, 1974).
58. Weiskopf, F. C., *Unter fremden Himmeln. Ein Abriß der deutschen
     Literatur im Exil, 1933-47* (Berlin, Dietz, 1948).
59. Wohlwill, Emil, *Galilei und sein Kampf für die copernicanische Lehre*,
     2 vols (Hamburg and Leipzig, L. Voss, 1909 and 1926).